Leading from the Library

Help Your School Community Thrive in the Digital Age

Shannon McClintock Miller
and William Bass

D1452998

International Society for Technology in Education
PORTLAND, OREGON • ARLINGTON, VIRGINIA

Leading from the Library
Help Your School Community Thrive in the Digital Age
Shannon McClintock Miller and William Bass

Editor: *Emily Reed*
Copy Editor: *Karstin Painter*
Proofreader: *Corinne Gould*
Indexer: *Wendy Allex*
Book Design and Production: *Kim McGovern*
Cover Design: *Edwin Ouellette*

Library of Congress Cataloging-in-Publication Data

Names: Miller, Shannon (Shannon McClintock), author. | Bass,
    William L., 1973- author.
Title: Leading from the library : help your school community thrive in
    the digital age / Shannon McClintock Miller and William Bass.
Description: First edition. | Portland, Oregon : International Society
    for Technology in Education, [2019] | Includes bibliographical
    references and index.
Identifiers: LCCN 2019000377 (print) | LCCN 2019006638 (ebook) |
    ISBN 9781564847072 (epub) | ISBN 9781564847065 (mobi) | ISBN
    9781564847089 (pdf) | ISBN 9781564847096 (pbk.)
Subjects: LCSH: School libraries—United States. | Libraries
    and schools—United States. | School libraries—Information
    technology—United States. | School librarian participation in
    curriculum planning—United States. | School librarians—Effect of
    technological innovations on—United States. | Education—Effect of
    technological innovations on—United States.
Classification: LCC Z675.S3 (ebook) | LCC Z675.S3 M378 2019 (print) |
    DDC 027.80973—dc23
LC record available at https://lccn.loc.gov/2019000377

First Edition
ISBN: 978-1-56484-709-6
Ebook version available.

ISTE® is a registered trademark of the International Society for
Technology in Education.

About ISTE

The International Society for Technology in Education (ISTE) is the premier nonprofit organization serving educators and education leaders committed to empowering connected learners in a connected world. ISTE serves more than 100,000 education stakeholders throughout the world.

ISTE's innovative offerings include the ISTE Conference & Expo, one of the biggest, most comprehensive ed tech events in the world—as well as the widely adopted ISTE Standards for learning, teaching and leading in the digital age and a robust suite of professional learning resources, including webinars, online courses, consulting services for schools and districts, books, and peer-reviewed journals and publications. Visit iste.org to learn more.

Related ISTE Titles

The Digital Citizenship Handbook for School Leaders
by Mike Ribble and Marty Park (2019)

The Edtech Advocate's Guide to Leading Change in Schools
by Mark Gura (2018)

Education Reimagined: Leading Systemwide Change with the ISTE Standards
by Helen Crompton (2018)

To see all books available from ISTE, visit iste.org/Books.

Digital Age Librarians Series

This series written for librarians by librarians features books focused on topics important to media specialists/teacher librarians.

Reimagining Library Spaces: Transform Your Space on Any Budget
by Diana Rendina
> This practical guide shares tips for affordably transforming library spaces, how-tos for hosting makerspaces and learning labs, and suggestions for supporting BYOD.

Connected Librarians: Tap Social Media to Enhance Professional Development and Student Learning
by Nikki D Robertson
> This engaging book provides the professional development librarians need to understand how to use social media effectively to improve student learning.

Inspiring Curiosity: The Librarian's Guide to Inquiry-Based Learning
by Colette Cassinelli
> This practical guide for secondary school librarians details how to collaborate with teachers and students to develop inquiry-based research projects.

About the Authors

Shannon McClintock Miller is the K–12 district teacher librarian at Van Meter Community School District in Iowa. She also serves as the Future Ready Librarian spokesperson with Follett and the Alliance for Excellent Education and international speaker and consultant. Shannon is the author of the award winning blog, The Library Voice, and 12 children's books about libraries and Makerspaces with Capstone. In 2013, she was named one of the Faces of Innovation by Broadband for America, was one of 50 people featured in the 2013 Center for Digital Education Yearbook and was a featured Connected Educator with the Connected Educators projects in partnership with the U.S. Department of Education. In 2014, she was named a Library Journal Mover and Shaker, and in 2016, she was awarded the ISTE Making IT Happen Award, and in 2018, Shannon was named the AASL Leadership Luminary Social Media Superstar. But her best job of all is being a mom to Brianna, Brady and Hagan, and wife to Eric.

William Bass is the innovation coordinator for instructional technology, information and library media for the Parkway School District in St. Louis, Missouri, and is president of the ISTE Board of Directors. As a nationally recognized education leader, he has received a number of awards including being named as one of the "20 to Watch" educational technology leaders from the National School Board

Association and awarded the ISTE Making IT Happen Award. Throughout his more than 20-year career in education, he has held positions as a middle and high school English teacher, technology integration specialist, instructional coach and educational consultant. As a speaker, writer and professional developer, he focuses on systemic and sustainable integration of technology into classrooms at all grade levels and seeks to empower students and teachers with authentic learning experiences. He strives to continue to support and push school library programs to meet the needs of their students and communities and to recognize the role of technology, innovation, and information in the digital age. He is also the author of two other books and countless articles on the role of technology in education.

Acknowledgments

This book is the culmination of years of thinking, leading, and learning about what leadership looks like in school libraries. While there are far too many people to thank personally here, we first want to recognize all of the school leaders and teacher librarians who are paving the way and inspiring their students every day. These individuals and programs have shown us that libraries have a very bright future in our schools and communities and that we need librarians now more than ever to help us understand the flood of information with which we interact. First and foremost, we want to thank those who contributed to this book through their stories, their quotes, and the ideas that they have shared with us. We recognize that we stand before greatness when it comes to these individuals and know that we would not have been able to do this without them.

We also want to be sure to jointly thank some very special individuals that have pushed our thinking and been a guide in our work. Britten Follett and Follett Learning have been an amazing supporter of school libraries and the work that we have done individually and together. The Future Ready Schools program has been instrumental in our efforts to lead through the library and create opportunities for students in our schools and those schools with whom we work.

For Bill, he would first like to recognize the librarians and other leaders in the Parkway School District. Their willingness to trust him, try new things, embrace innovation, and look beyond their current reality has been astounding. They are an amazing group and Bill is honored to have the pleasure of working with them. He would also like to thank Kim Lindskog for her tireless efforts and partnership in leading the Parkway library program. Her insights into the role of librarians in the digital age and her strategic guidance have made all the difference. Amy Johnson, those in library services, and the entire Parkway Teaching, Learning and Accountability department have supported Bill in his work beyond Parkway in ways that they don't even know. They have provided inspiration and encouragement while acting as listening partners and friends with some humor built in. Lastly, Bill wants to thank his family for their patience and support through this process and throughout his entire career.

For Shannon, she would like to recognize all of the amazing kids she has worked with as a teacher librarian. They have inspired her daily and have shown her so many ways that student voice can make a difference in the library, school community, and throughout the world. She would also like to thank all of the teachers and administrators that she has worked with over the last 12 years at Van Meter Community School. They have been willing to collaborate, take chances and risks, and try out new things, offering wonderful opportunities, lots of fun times and special friendships. To embrace and celebrate all of the changes that are taking place within education, puts in perspective the open mindfulness, and ambition of the community within Van Meter.. Shannon would also like to thank her global community of colleagues and friends. Through her work across the country and internationally, she has learned so much and will forever be grateful for these opportunities, experiences and friendships. And most importantly, Shannon wants to thank her family for their support, guidance and love they give her everyday.

Finally, we would like to thank ISTE and the entire publishing team for giving us the opportunity to share our stories and bring this much needed book to the industry. We look forward to our future endeavors and are proud of the work that we have done together.

Dedication

Bill would like to dedicate this book to his wife, Kim, and children, Max and Molly, for their support and inspiration in this and all of his endeavors. He also wants to thanks his parents, Bill and Carol, and sister Cheri for all the times that they helped push him past hurdles to achieve his goals.

Shannon would like to dedicate this book to her three children, Brianna, Brady and Hagan; her husband Eric, and her parents, Paul and Rhonda, for their constant love, support and encouragement. And a special thanks to her sister, Heather, who she continues to "play" library and school with her after all these years.

Contents

Contents

Foreword

Over the past decade, many school libraries have undergone radical transformation. What was traditionally viewed as a quiet place where noise was frowned upon, is now often viewed as one of the main learning hubs, a fun place to be, and the heart of the school community. For hundreds of years, literacy has been the focus of libraries, and today's modern libraries are laser-focused on keeping literacy at the heart of learning. Yet, today's modern libraries also include flexible spaces for additional authentic and personal learning opportunities. It's not about choosing between literacy or innovative opportunities. It's about teaching literacy through innovative opportunities. Whether it's a makerspace, a coding corner, an exploration hub, or a creation station where students learn through iteration and the use of design software and a 3D printer, today's Future Ready libraries are engaging, interactive, and built upon deep levels of learning. They are no longer only places of consumption, but places of curation, creation, and design. Whether it's curled up getting lost in a book, or coding their way to solving problems, today's Future Ready libraries are a place kids want to be!

What I love most about the book that you're about to dive into is the way Shannon, a teacher librarian, and Bill, a district level administrator, both nationally respected leaders in the field, passionately focus on "the why," while helping us understand "the what" and "the how." Through a compilation of success stories from around the nation, and armed with the latest, cutting-edge resources, *Leading from the Library* will guide your transformation journey and help you meet the myriad of needs of today's readers and tomorrow's world leaders.

Shannon and Bill recognize that all communities are different; each with their own strengths and cultures. They recognize that what may work in one community, may look fundamentally different in another, and that's part of the strength of this book. Whether it's sharing out the incredible things happening every day in your library and becoming a dynamic advocate for the vital work, or transforming lessons to be relevant for today's modern learners, the best librarians lead ... right where they are.

Throughout these pages, you'll also feel a compelling call to action. This work isn't simply about celebrating great things that do happen. It's about creating the conditions for needed change, advocating for the work, and as librarians, making it happen. This could not be any more clear as Shannon and Bill tackle some very difficult issues, such as the rampant equity issues that remain prevalent in our schools. These issues are real. They are issues we are morally obligated to address. Our traditionally underserved students need and deserve every opportunity, and librarians are one of the keys to helping close this equity gap. *Leading from the Library* isn't just about what we can do. It's about what we must do.

By threading together resources and frameworks from Future Ready Librarians®, to the ISTE Standards, to Project Connect, Shannon and Bill leverage evidence-based tools to help us create the needed innovative culture in our libraries, while providing a roadmap to help guide us along the way, so that ultimately, we are empowered to lead, right now, from where we are. Leadership and school culture lay the foundation of schools that are Future Ready, and as such, your leadership, and the culture that you create, lay the foundation of creating the Future Ready Libraries that our students both need and deserve!

Have fun on your journey. Celebrate in your many successes and fail forward along the way. Together, we can do this!

All for the kids we serve,

Thomas C. Murray, Director of Innovation, Future Ready Schools®. Best-selling coauthor of *Learning Transformed: 8 Keys to Designing Tomorrow's Schools, Today*

Introduction

We spoke to librarians and school leaders across the United States, and they shared a common feeling about the role of libraries in the digital age: It seems to be constantly in flux. The digital age has brought revolutionary new tools that have impacted our schools and libraries in dramatic ways. Access to devices and the internet has improved both at home and in our classrooms and we are utilizing digital content to engage students in meaningful ways. Contrary to the misguided beliefs of some, the work of the librarian is not merely reading books to kids and helping them check out materials. It never was. Modern librarians are curators of information, tools, and strategies; they see everyone who walks through the doors of their schools as a potential learner. They are masters of technology and understand the way computers and the internet have changed how we both use and value information. These are the librarians of the digital age.

Common perception may paint a picture of librarians as one dimensional, as only curators. We recognize that, to be effective, librarians must go far beyond resources and materials, finding "just right books," and teaching research. In the digital age, librarians must respond to the challenges of the existing world and try to predict what the future will hold. In short, librarians must be leaders in the fields of education, technology, and information and be both willing and able to share their expertise. Only by embracing that leadership will we be able to begin to repaint the picture and change perceptions.

That's why this book exists. We hope to share our insight, experience, and stories to empower change in our schools and solidify digital age library programs through the leadership of our school librarians.

Project Connect, Future Ready Schools, ISTE Standards and Librarians

In our work, we are regularly asked for advice and guidance about the changes that librarians and schools want to make in their library programs. In these cases, we point to a number of guiding documents that have helped us to pave the way for the changes that we want to see in our own programs. While not an exclusive list, Project Connect, Future Ready Schools, and the ISTE Standards provide structure for change and an understanding of the role of the digital age librarian. These three documents are the basis for the changes that we have made in our own schools and what we often point librarians to in their own work. As an administrator responsible for his library program at a district level, Bill uses these documents as a way to have common language with his librarians to make tangible change in the programming, mindset, and spaces that make up those school libraries. Throughout the book we will reference each of these documents many times, citing examples and approaches that we have seen make change to programs around the country.

Project Connect

Every career and program has defining moments that change one's thinking enough to alter the direction and approach to one's work. This happened for Bill in 2015, when he attended the American Associations of School Librarians (AASL) National Conference in Columbus, Ohio. He was in his third year serving as the district administrator responsible for the school library program, and he accidentally wandered into a superintendent panel being moderated by Britten Follett, senior vice president of marketing strategy and classroom initiatives at Follett School

Solutions. During that session, she was describing the Project Connect framework that had been put together to redefine libraries and prepare them for the realities of a modern library programs. As he was listening to the speakers, it became clear that this was the guiding document that he had been looking for to do some long-term planning for his district. He was inspired and motivated by the framework and immediately began looking for more information.

If you are unfamiliar with Project Connect, it is a framework developed by Follett "to advocate for librarians as district leaders so that students can learn digital literacy, modern research techniques and cutting-edge skills that apply across all subject areas" (Follett Learning, 2015). This framework can be used as a guiding document for schools and districts to set goals, communicate the role of a modern librarian and library program, and provide a structure for professional learning for librarians seeking to grow in their practice. More specifically, Project Connect breaks the role of the librarian into nine different facets that define and explain the role of the digital age librarian. Brigid Dolan, a high school librarian in Bill's district, says that Project Connect

> ...defined the different roles we play in our schools and helped us think about how we spend our time and what we do on a daily basis. It categorizes our work and helps to give us language that we can use that is understandable by everyone. In my library, it's helped me to communicate with my teachers and community to let them know all the ways that I can be helpful for them.

If you're just starting with Project Connect, we suggest taking a look at the framework (found at **tiny.cc/hllr2y**) and completing the inventory worksheet in Table 0.1 (an editable version of this document can also be found at **tiny.cc/2llr2y**). This breaks down each of the Project Connect elements and helps you analyze the work that you do over the course of a week. While some of the topics definitely overlap, this will give you a picture of how you spend your time as a librarian and where your opportunities are to redefine the work that you do.

TABLE 0.1 | Project Connect Inventory Worksheet

TOPIC	CURRENTLY DOING *Where do you see this in your current work?*	WANT TO DO *Where could you fit this in?*
Professional Development		
Instructional Partnership		
Digital Citizenship		
Curriculum and Technology Integration		
Information Literacy		
Content access and curation		
Reading and literacy advocacy		
Learning space design/ making and building (4Cs)		
Equity		

Source: Kim Lindskog, Parkway School District

Upon his return from AASL, Bill began looking further into the origins of Project Connect and eventually connected with Sara Trettin from the U.S. Office of Educational Technology, who was working on an early draft of what would become the Future Ready Librarians® Framework with the U.S. Department of Education. While this was early in the lives of both documents, the potential for change was immediately evident, and the connection to the work that many districts were doing became the catalyst that he needed to rethink how libraries could be structured and approached in his district.

Future Ready Librarians® Framework

Future Ready Schools was part of the U.S. White House ConnectED Initiative that was launched in 2014, where district superintendents from around the country came together to launch their transition to digital learning and sign the Future Ready District Pledge. That event became a catalyst for change in schools to prepare them to meet the needs of students, now and in the future. During this time, Follett and the U.S. Department of Education had partnered to develop the Future Ready Librarians® Framework.

According to Britten Follett,

> The conversation started around creating a standard for a librarian's job description and revisiting the rubric by which librarians are evaluated. But we quickly determined that wasn't enough. So we created the Future Ready Librarians® Framework as a way of connecting the dots between the role of a library and a librarian to the challenges districts are facing. Every Future Ready librarian's role might look different depending on the strategic needs of the district. (Personal Communication, 2018)

With the help of Follett and a number of librarians from across the country, Future Ready Librarians® was the first framework created as a part of the Future Ready Schools Initiative. It also serves as a guiding document for library programs as they connect their work with that of their overall districts. What makes this framework so useful is the parallel structure with Future Ready Schools. Because the overarching topics are the same, it brings consistent language to schools and libraries, moving them in the same direction toward supporting each other. This structure and alignment signifies the importance of the librarian to the overall school environment and helps to further solidify the librarian as a leader in our schools. Since its initial development, the framework has undergone a second iteration and now includes the element of literacy as central to the work of the librarian.

Shannon has been involved in these initiatives from the very beginning and has been fortunate to support and provide ongoing development for librarians, as well as advocate for these guiding documents in schools across the world. In 2017, she had the opportunity to become the library spokesperson for Future Ready Librarians® and Project Connect. It was one of those opportunities she couldn't refuse, and she is forever thankful to have had a role in amplifying the message of both programs.

Throughout the book, we regularly reference the Future Ready Librarians® Framework and refer to the "wedges" that make direct ties between the categories and libraries. These wedges provide the basis for connections between what is considered traditional library work and district and administrator goals. We specifically focus on how librarians can lead beyond the library, but we also recognize that every element in the Future Ready "wheel" (Figure 0.1) includes some leadership capacity.

As you explore this Future Ready Librarians® wheel, pay close attention to the edges of each of the wedges and take note that each one of them starts with an action. As we've already stated, opportunities for leadership abound in this framework, and those actions are where it starts. Just like with Project Connect, we recommend taking inventory of your current practice and identifying the opportunities that can come in these categories. You may have to be creative in your thinking, but opportunities are everywhere, and these are topics that administrators think about on a regular basis. If, as a librarian, you use this consistent language, your work will be crystal clear in its alignment to the work of the greater school community.

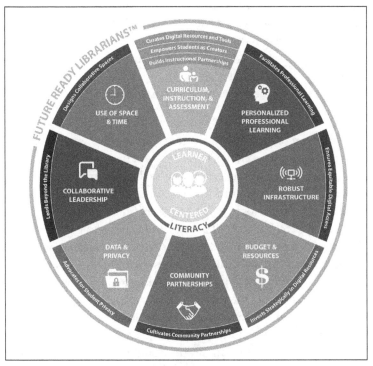

Figure 0.1. Future Ready Librarians® wheel.
Source: Alliance for Excellent Education, Future Ready Schools, and Future Ready Librarians®, reprinted with permission.

For more information about the Future Ready Schools and Future Ready Librarians® Frameworks as well as webinars, events and other resources, visit **futureready.org**. On this site is a wealth of information and resources that can help you frame the conversation with your administrators.

ISTE Standards

The final guiding document that we like to focus on when we are considering how librarians are leaders is the ISTE Standards. The family of ISTE Standards includes that of student, educator, leader, coach, and computer science educators and has been the go to resource for teachers who use technology since its inception. Originally released as the National Educational Technology Standards (NETS) in 1998, these standards quickly became a guiding force for schools around the country (and the world) as schools began to make serious investments in technology for student use.

If we focus in on only the Student Standards, it's remarkable to see how they have changed as they have been refreshed. In earlier iterations, they reflected what skills we wanted students to acquire, what we wanted them to do and how we wanted them to approach technology. When they were updated in 2016, the focus shifted to focus on who we want students to be and tied the standards more to mindset and their learning than discrete skills. That shift significantly changes the nature of what a set of standards can actually mean and provides a natural entry point for librarians as they identify resources and collaborate with teachers to create intentionally designed lessons that will draw each of the seven standards out of students. Additionally, the Standards for Educators and Educational Leaders have also been refreshed and are aligned to the student standards supporting the case that, if we want our students to meet these technology standards, adults must do the same.

One of the resources that have been created specifically to help librarians meet the ISTE Standards for Educators is a crosswalk between the standards and the Future Ready Librarians® Framework. This document (which can be found at **tiny.cc/4lur2y**) was released in 2018 in partnership between ISTE, Follett, and the Alliance for Excellent Education in order to help librarians see the distinct connections between the two and find the correlations to the one with which they are most familiar in order to deepen their understanding of each of them. The goals of the crosswalk are to help librarians find new approaches to teaching and learning through leadership and to offer ongoing support for teachers and students.

If we want our students to meet these technology standards, adults must do the same.

We will reference the ISTE Standards many times throughout this book, but if you'd like to know more, visit **iste.org/standards** to download and explore all the standards and their resources.

Our Stories

We first met in the Bloggers' Cafe at the 2008 National Educational Computing Conference (NECC) in San Antonio, Texas. At that time, Shannon was a school librarian in Van Meter, Iowa, and Bill was a technology integration specialist in St. Louis, Missouri. During our brief conversation, we shared our excitement about attending the event that was the precursor to the ISTE EdTech Conference as we know it today. Since that moment, we have kept in touch, often seeing each other at events and interacting online. Our shared work with Project Connect and the Future Ready Librarians® Framework brought us together for this partnership.

In her role as librarian at Van Meter Community School District, Shannon was constantly looking for opportunities to connect her own students with other students and experts outside of her library and school community. It became evident that she needed to create a blog that could share the story of her library while highlighting her students' work. The Library Voice (**vanmeterlibraryvoice.blogspot.com**) was born. Through this blog and social media, Shannon discussed learning, technology, reading, creating, and collaborating in a way that helped other schools look for creative approaches to engage students. By partnering with other Van Meter district leaders, she positioned the library as an influential force in her district and quickly became a leader in the field. Shannon's work has led her in many directions, but her focus continues to be serving as a voice for library programs around the world.

Bill's route to empowering leadership through libraries took a different path. As a former high school English teacher, literacy and literature have always been lenses through which he sees the world. Many of the emerging technologies that we now take for granted were introduced during his years in the classroom. Recognizing the potential of utilizing these tools for learning, he began to seek out and embed technology and digital tools into his practice. An early adopter of podcasting and blogs, he was intrigued by the way that technology could impact learning. He quickly recognized that the world was changing; the very definition of what it meant to be literate would need to be reconsidered. After leaving the classroom in 2007, Bill served on the Executive Committee for the National Council of Teachers of English and was a part of the group that created the Definition for Twenty-First Century Literacies as well as the Framework for Twenty-First Century Curriculum and Assessment. This experience solidified his resolve to focus on literacy in all of its forms in his role as a technology integration specialist, where he was responsible for coaching and developing teachers in their practice. After six years working with teachers as a technology and instructional coach, he moved into district administration and took over the instructional technology and library programs in his district. He began to consider how to systemically position librarians as natural leaders in their schools and beyond.

What's In This Book?

For the purposes of this book, we think it's important to recognize that we all lead from our own spaces. Shannon, as a practicing librarian, has a very different perspective than that of Bill, a district administrator. However, leadership is about influence and creating conditions for success. It's about recognizing the opportunities that abound in school libraries and making the most of them to bring about changes that will empower and support your students as learners. Whether you're a librarian or an administrator, libraries can serve as a catalyst for change and, if harnessed, can become the one of the most important connectors in a building. Leadership doesn't have a destination; it's always shifting. It's not attaining a specific position, gaining social media followers, or becoming a professional speaker. Leadership is about creating conditions to move forward in our work and to unlock the potential of librarians to partner with and support teaching and learning in schools.

Throughout this book we will share stories and strategies that we have used ourselves, or that we have seen effectively implemented in various library programs. While each chapter stands on its own, there is also a great deal of overlap among chapters. There is no one "right way" to advance leadership through library programs. Rather, advancing leadership requires a multilayered approach that involves strategic thinking and intentional decision making. It's an ongoing process that asks us to consider the big picture and long-term goals as opposed to immediate gains and low-impact activities.

Here is what the reader will find in each chapter:

Chapter 1 discusses how to build, maintain, and foster trust and relationships with administrators, teachers, and the greater school community. These individual groups have important roles in supporting educational efforts in our schools. We emphasize the unique position of librarians to serve as digital age mentors to the community by helping both students and adults navigate the intricacies of the digital world.

Chapter 2 focuses on the unique community that constitutes every school. We recognize that not every strategy in this book will work in every location; librarians influence their communities in a variety of ways. However, by focusing on the culture of the school and greater communities, we can give students greater opportunities and experiences.

Chapter 3 addresses advocacy and encourages readers to find and tell their stories. Here, we identify strategies for amplifying student voices and connecting the work of the library to the greater community.

Chapter 4 explores how librarians lead through their curriculum and lessons on what it means to be literate in the digital age. It highlights the importance of partnering with teachers to meet the needs of the school community.

Chapter 5 is meant as a call to action for all readers to be a force for change in their communities and to embrace leadership for the benefit of all students.

Inside these chapters you will find references to stories from the field as well as resources and strategies for implementation. Finally, each chapter includes questions that can be used as prompts for book studies, professional learning communities, or other learning opportunities for librarians.

#LeadingLibs Challenge

At the end of each chapter, you will find a series of challenges to get you started with the topics we cover. These challenges are meant to provide you with an opportunity to push yourself in your leadership role. For some of you, these challenges may be things you're already doing. If that's the case, that's amazing, and we appreciate all your work! However, we also encourage you to consider how you can challenge yourself using that topic. How can you take your work a step further and encourage those around you to grow?

If this is new for you, we understand that too. We are all in different places in our work. As we stated earlier, leadership is not a destination and neither is your library program. There will always be room for improvement and change. Use these prompts to help you get started.

Post these challenges to your favorite community using the hashtag #LeadingLibs, and follow one another's journey so we can share, strategize, and learn from each other.

- Join one of the various librarian and educational communities that are available online (e.g., ISTE, AASL, your local state library organization) and connect with librarians outside of your community.

- Download a copy of the Future Ready Librarians® Framework (**FutureReady.org**) and share it with a library colleague (in or out of your school community).

- Join the Future Ready Librarians® Facebook group (**facebook.com/groups/futurereadylibrarians**) and engage with that community about what you find most exciting in your library.

- Explore the case studies published by Project Connect (**follettlearning.com/projectconnect**).

- Participate in a Twitter chat such as #FutureReadyLibs and #TLchat.

CHAPTER 1

Digital Age Mentors

We are very good at associating librarians with our past,
but the question is, do you see them as a part of the future?

   —MARK RAY, (TEDx, 2016)

Information and digital tools are changing at an amazing pace, and there are a great many unknowns in the world. Teachers, parents, administrators, and students are looking for guidance on how to navigate this ever-changing technological landscape. Let's be honest, keeping up with technological advances is not just tough, it's impossible. Every day there are new tools, websites, and services jockeying for our attention, offering fantastic new ways to accomplish tasks, learn content, or simply be entertained. Whether you see it as digital distraction or essential information, this continuous shift in knowledge creates an opportunity for librarians to be digital age mentors, cultivating digital skills, online learning, and understanding of the information age.

Being a digital age mentor involves more than tools and content. It's about leadership and finding those opportunities to lead. Sometimes that means that you spearhead new initiatives, while other times your colleagues take the lead and you provide guidance by supporting them in their endeavors. Regardless, being a leader means that you look for—and seize—those opportunities that will have the most impact on your community while meeting the needs of your students.

But how do you actually mentor others and lead in this space when the landscape of digital tools and access is constantly shifting? Let's be clear, being a digital age mentor is hard work; it takes a commitment to continuous learning and exploration. You must be flexible, recognize patterns and trends in tools and content, and look at the broader picture of education, information, and libraries. Above all, you must position yourself as a partner and a leader in your school community.

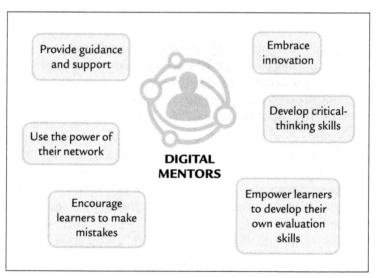

Figure 1.1. What digital mentors do

In both of our programs, we rely on the ISTE Standards for Students as a guiding document for our work. It bears repeating that these newly revised standards change the focus from what we want students to do to who we want them to be. With that shift, the new ISTE Standards for teachers and administrators are tied directly to students; we can make progress toward the Student Standards only by seeing the role of educators and leaders in new ways. Librarians fit into both of these categories, so it's crucial for them to have a deep understanding of how the various ISTE Standards fit together.

Connecting the Leader Standard

Let's look more closely at the Leader Standard in the 2017 Educator Standards in light of the library and digital age mentorship.

STANDARD 2. LEADER

Educators seek out opportunities for leadership to support student empowerment and success and to improve teaching and learning.

That phrase should strike librarians as a critical piece of their day-to-day work. A digital age mentor's work does not start when students walk into the library space, nor does it manifest itself only in the lessons and learning experiences you design for your students. It's about your entire approach—how you think about your time and your influence in the communities (school and beyond) that you serve.

INDICATOR 2.A

Shape, advance and accelerate a shared vision for empowered learning with technology by engaging with education stakeholders.

Partnerships with influential people in your school community are crucial to defining this shared vision. Again, this ties directly into mentorship and the Community Partnerships wedge of the Future

Ready Librarians® Framework. The more opportunities that you can create to engage and connect with teachers, parents, students, and others who impact your school community, the more likely you will influence that vision and advance it through your library program. Being a digital mentor isn't simply about mentoring students; it's also about fostering a shared vision in the community.

INDICATOR 2.B

Advocate for equitable access to educational technology, digital content, and learning opportunities to meet the diverse needs of all students.

While it may seem obvious, advocating for students is a big part of what librarians do as digital age mentors. In many cases, schools have created barriers to digital content and learning experiences for our students. It's well meaning and often done with the intent of keeping students "safe." Libraries have always been places meant to open doors and minds for our students and to give them opportunities to explore, create, and experience worlds that are sometimes shut off or inaccessible. This indicator gets to the heart of the role librarians play in our schools. Through partnerships, librarians push teachers and administrators to level the playing field for students and remove some of the barriers that inhibit learning and help to prepare them for their lives outside of our schools

INDICATOR 2.C.

Model for colleagues the identification, exploration, evaluation, curation, and adoption of new digital resources and tools for learning.

This last indicator in the Leader Standard also speaks to how librarians are taking on the role of professional developer and provides structure for the instructional partnerships that are so important in our schools. As digital age mentors, we must keep in mind that it's not about what is new and shiny; it's about the tools and resources that are key to learning, and how teachers use them to design authentic learning experiences for students. In her book, *Learning First, Technology Second*, Liz Kolb reminds us that "the instructional choices that teachers make when integrating technology will determine how deeply students are embedded in the learning process and their long-term retention of the content goals in the experience" (2017, p. 16). The same holds true for adults. As librarians and administrators work together, the models they create around digital resources and tools become increasingly important to student impact and learning in the classroom. An intentional approach can go a long way toward adoption of any digital tool. Knowing the right time and place to introduce something is critical, and it is a reflection of how well you understand the culture of your school community. In chapter 2, we discuss the importance of librarians being in tune with their school's culture when leading.

While we have spent some time here exploring Standard 2, it is obviously not the only one relevant to leading through the library. However, the leader standard is critical to transformative strides in improving the educational experience of students, especially when we consider the librarian as a digital age mentor. Each of the Educator Standards speak to library programs in different ways, but all tie back to the Student Standards and preparing the whole child to live in the digital age.

The Power of Relationships

The key to digital age mentorship is to create relationships that foster partnerships both in and out of school. These relationships are crucial components to mentoring all learners in your school community, and they can make or break library programs. One of the keys to a successful library and literacy program has always been knowing one's students as readers. We go to great lengths to learn about their interests, their habits, and their ideas. We want to understand how we can serve them best, and we want to share our love of reading, books, and technology. While not all of these student relationships are forged easily, they are founded because students come to the library with their teachers, or on their own, and we can ask questions and explore with them. The relationships we build with students are unique in that we can offer a safe place where they can explore and discover who they are through books.

Developing strong relationships with students is just one piece of a far bigger puzzle. In our schools, and with good reason, libraries are often seen as the hubs. They are the spaces where we get help, find information, and explore topics that we find interesting. They are comfortable, inviting, and exciting. When students walk in, they never know what they might be met with in a constantly changing environment. In school libraries, we cater to students and form our relationships based on them. But what about adults? Our school communities include a combination of learners, and everyone should be seen as a potential learner. Parents, teachers, administrators, business owners or community leaders—each of these groups represent learners who are potentially seeking guidance and support. These are the people with whom we need to build relationships and for whom we need to act as digital age mentors.

Students

The first, and most obvious, group of people that you should seek to mentor is students. As they find their way in the world, they are met with expectations and challenges unique to their generation. However, being born in the digital age and having access to technology does not mean they have a deep understanding of how technology works or impacts them, and they are often limited in their usage by adults. They are explorers of the digital world but don't see it as magic. They have grown up with these technologies in an era where many of the adults they look to don't understand the way that the internet and quick and easy access to information and efficiencies that come with technology are engrained in their lives. They need someone (maybe a librarian) to share their digital lives and discuss the decisions they make regarding technology and digital tools. That doesn't mean that we need another full lesson plan about internet safety or digital citizenship, but rather we need to engage our students in discussions about usage, responsibility and decision making. It could actually be as simple as talking about why we, as adults, chooses specific keywords for a search while you are making the search. In this case, we are simply modeling the decisions we make rather than assuming that our students will get it or respond to that one lesson plan where we discuss it. We are desperately in need of mentors, even if our students won't admit it.

STUDENT STRATEGIES

- Ask students what digital tools they are currently using.
- Connect library lessons with classroom learning.
- Talk with students about the decisions you make as a user of technology.
- Give students an opportunity to try a new tool and then teach you how to use it.

Teachers and Staff

One of the most important adult relationships that librarians can foster is with teachers and staff in their school or district. Classrooms are where students spend the majority of their days, and we rely on teachers to partner with us so we have access to those students. We are all in this together; no single person in a school is the sole teacher of any given student. There are also amazing demands on teachers and staff. We are all responsible for curriculum, behavior, after school activities, and overall school climate and culture. Librarians support these elements of schools and can have a dramatic impact on their communities, but much of their work happens behind the scenes and may not be directly related to the lessons taught in the library. A librarian's contribution might come in the form of conversations that happen in hallways, professional development during lunch, or co-planning a lesson to connect the library to curriculum.

Stacia Wagers, a librarian at Shenandoah Valley Elementary in Bill's district, spends her time every day before school doing what she refers to as "five minutes of harassment," where she checks in with her teachers to learn about their curricular plans for the week. By intentionally connecting with all her teachers, she has positioned herself as a supporting member of their grade-level teams. She mentors them by identifying digital tools and practices that will engage their students in meaningful usage of technology. When it comes to building partnerships, Stacia sees this as the most important five minutes of her day, and her teachers have responded because they see it as a way to support student learning in the classroom.

We like to think about these intentional connections as the influence that librarians have on their school environments. Every decision that is made for a library program should be strategic, in support of students and the teachers and staff who work with them. As you build these relationships, more opportunities for collaboration will naturally present themselves. We acknowledge that this can be a hard road. There are those in schools who do not want that kind of support. However, we owe it to our students to move beyond adult barriers and support learners regardless of adult interactions. Whenever either of us work with new librarians in a school, we try to impress upon them that the entire first year of their work should focus on building relationships. Sometimes that means finding those small wins and finding that one person with whom you can work can make all the difference.

TEACHER AND STAFF STRATEGIES

- Find natural partnerships as a starting point and expand from there.

- Advertise what you can do for your teachers. If they don't know what you have to offer, they won't approach you to collaborate.

- Maintain a focus on student learning. Teachers want their students working toward curricular goals.

- Continue your support of literacy and reading appreciation in the school.

- Offer just-in-time learning opportunities (e.g., lunch and learns, after-school workshops) to showcase new technologies or strategies that will help teachers and their students.

Parents

The relationship librarians have with parents is multifaceted, and it shifts as students move through their schooling. In the early years, we are partners in literacy with both our students and their parents. We seek opportunities to bring excitement to reading and provide parents with the tools and strategies to help their kids learn to read. As students get older, we are still partners and work to keep reading in their lives, but we expand our role to include media and information literacy, critical thinking, and research.

Nikki D Robertson is a librarian at Winkley Elementary School in Leander, Texas and author of the ISTE book *Connected Librarians: Tap Social Media to Enhance Professional Development* (2017). She shares a story about one of the ways that she has been able to connect with parents this year and bring a piece of the library to them.

While it may seem simple, this connection creates trust and helps parents partner with Nikki and her fellow librarians to teach students how to be responsible for their books and materials.

LIBRARIAN PERSPECTIVE

Nikki D Robertson

Forming partnerships with parents has been a big focus for me this year. One of the most frustrating things for a parent is getting late book notifications. As our library operates on a six day fixed color rotation schedule, the ability to easily know when your child goes to the library is a confusing and frustrating labyrinth. To communicate with parents directly, I use the Remind App (**remind.com**). If their child's library day is on a purple day, a Remind notification is sent directly to their cell phone the night before reminding parents to help their child get their books in their backpacks. I also post color day reminders through our school library social media accounts. I've had many parents tell me how helpful these reminders are. Setting up these reminders is well worth the time invested and goes towards building a positive relationship with parents.

In the digital age, we must also provide guidance for parents and encourage them to be intentional with technology use. In Shannon's district, librarians are often called upon to work with local parent organizations to address topics such as screen time, video games, internet safety, and social media. She finds that parents want help because they are raising kids in an era that is dramatically different from the one in which they grew up. They are looking for answers and, while the internet is full of answers, they trust the experts at their local schools. This is a prime opportunity for librarians to build those relationships.

However, there is one caveat to this relationship. As parents ourselves, we know it's tough to be a parent when the world is changing so rapidly. Serving as a digital age mentor does not mean that you must have all the answers, and it certainly doesn't mean that you are the authority on parenting in the digital age. What it does mean is that you're willing and able to provide resources, stay current on trends that students care about, and most importantly, you're willing to engage in conversations with parents and support them as well as your students.

PARENT STRATEGIES

- Offer to present at PTO meetings around topics related to technology.
- Highlight families who volunteer in the library.
- Publicly showcase students who make positive decisions with their technology using a library webpage or social media account.

Administrators

It's no secret that administrators are busy people. They juggle all manner of initiatives and are often the public faces of schools or districts. They are disciplinarians, evaluators, instructional leaders, facility managers, politicians, public relations specialists ... the list goes on. Put simply, it's a seemingly impossible job. However, the unique demands of their positions make administrators prime candidates for partnering with librarians. They need someone to lead the tech committee or design a plan for addressing digital citizenship. They want their students to be successful and their parents to be happy. They want to meet their short- and long-term strategic goals and create excitement around learning. They need solutions to problems they didn't know they had, and they ultimately want to grow and foster a community so kids can learn. All that is to say, administrators need librarians for all the same reasons that parents, teachers, and students do. They need you to lead in ways that align with the school goals, and they need you to use your influence to create authentic, meaningful learning experiences for students.

ADMINISTRATOR STRATEGIES

- Present your administrator with a plan for how the library will support the school's goals.

- Create and maintain the school social media accounts to highlight what's happening with the school. Mentor your administrator by teaching them how to utilize those accounts as communication tools.

- Curate and develop resources for digital citizenship and media literacy to support teachers.

- Recognize your role not only in instruction but in the day-to-day running of the school and have a conversation with your administrator about how to most effectively use your time.

Community Members

Schools are a valuable community asset; they regularly partner with businesses and individuals to provide experiences and opportunities for students. As the digital world has expanded, so too has our community expanded beyond its geographical borders. This means that we must strike a balance between our local community and our extended community. Both communities have something to offer, and it's incumbent upon us to form relationships and leverage those to benefit our students in addition to giving back to those communities. This is part of what Lawrence Lessig, Roy L. Furman Professor of Law at Harvard Law School, refers to as the "sharing economy" in his book *Remix: Making Art and Commerce Thrive in the Hybrid Economy* (2008). In the digital age, part of the relationships that we form requires us to give as much, or more, than we take. Libraries are said to serve a greater good; they work to democratize information and its access. The relationships we create with our patrons and global communities only serve to reinforce the good we can do in the world. Those individuals or groups become the best advocates for our schools and for literacy in our communities.

It's not about how many students you reach by teaching an individual lesson, it's about the influence you have on your school community and how many students you can reach by reaching your teachers.

A few years ago, one of Bill's librarians, Leah Plumley of Highcroft Ridge Elementary, had a goal of connecting with her local community around literacy over the summer. She had offered library nights where families could check out books during the summer, but she knew some families would be unable to attend due to transportation or work schedules. To overcome those obstacles, and to build relationships with those families, she sought sponsors and partnerships with local apartment complexes to set up a mobile book library. Visiting the local neighborhoods on a weekly basis, she found a way to reach out to students and families, provide them with books and reading opportunities, and connect them to the school community during those summer months that school wasn't in session. Three years later, the book mobile is still going strong, and the idea has expanded into other parts of the district and other areas of the country.

This story illustrates the impact that a librarian can have on her community. This one project, meant to bring books to students, provided the school new and exciting partnerships with parents and community members. Leah is leading the way and serving as a steward of her school in her community and beyond. Digital age mentorship isn't always about the digital. It's about the era we find ourselves in and the changing nature of our schools and culture. It's about leadership, partnerships, and relationships. It's about critical thinking and solving problems. And it's about approaching our work in a way that builds and solidifies our influence in our communities.

STRATEGIES FOR BUILDING RELATIONSHIPS IN THE COMMUNITY

- Invite anyone who is willing to visit your library.

- Be proactive in making connections that will serve both the library program and your school community.

- Share beyond your current environment. The connections you make will bring dividends to your school.

Collaborative Connections

Collaboration is one of the skills required for literacy in today's world, and librarians are master collaborators. We see it in the co-planning of lessons and sharing of resources that impact what and how students learn. Collaboration is a skill that is honed over time, but it's also a skill that is central to library programs around the world.

Wielding Influence

It's not about how many students you reach by teaching an individual lesson, it's about the influence you have on your school community and how many students you can reach by reaching your teachers. In the Future Ready Librarians® Framework, the Facilitates Professional Learning and Cultivates Community Partnerships wedges present the need for librarians to consider how they will have the largest impact on their school communities.

In 2015, Bill's district offered more professional learning in an online format. Much like online programs and classes offered in higher education and some K–12 schools, this shift was meant to honor teachers' time and make learning more accessible, flexible, and relevant to classroom practice. As the offerings matured, Bill sought opportunities for librarians to create classes for teachers on topics such as information and media literacy. There was some initial concern because many of these courses highlighted teacher–librarian collaboration. If we continued to offer these types of courses, would we sabotage collaborative opportunities and render librarians unnecessary? While there is truth in that fear, and the potential is there, the need for a teacher-librarian partnership won't be replaced, but rather, further enhanced because there will be time to focus on the other needs of the school and the classroom. The conversation quickly shifted to how we can best serve the needs of our students as opposed to keeping information sacred. We moved beyond the fear that sharing information would risk our positions, but that shift in thinking was necessary to move forward and offer these classes.

This shift in the library curriculum is occurring in many districts. In 2017, Parkway's library program underwent an evaluation that is helping to refocus and shape the program. The evaluation utilized the ISTE Standards, Future Ready Librarians® and Schools Frameworks, and Follett's Project Connect as guiding documents for what the library program could be and engaged district librarians and the Parkway community by seeking to answer one question: What does it mean to be a librarian in the digital age? Through a series of interviews, a community open forum, student focus groups, and surveys, the group sought to study the following topics:

- Role of the librarian

- Digital strategies and content

- Student choice and personalization

- Flexible programming

- Literacy advocacy

Obviously there are many elements under each of these topics which were studied along the way. The methodology, findings, and recommendations are all outlined in the final report which can be found at **parkwayschools.net/Page/4422**. As a result of this evaluation, one of the findings was that the program needed to update the library curriculum to be sure that it was flexible, relevant, and met the needs of students. Two of the recommendations are specifically relevant to the idea of collaboration and digital mentoring causing our librarians that are a part of the program to think differently about their instruction and what we teach. They recognized that their "curriculum" is really the curriculum of the entire district and that they must support what is going on in classrooms. That doesn't mean that they stop teaching, but it does mean that they must be more collaborative and think about the entire student body as opposed to individual classes. It means that they will be more intentional about working with teachers to align library lessons and skills to what's happening in the classroom. It also means that it doesn't really matter who teaches an individual lesson, rather, it matters that it is taught. It means that they must shift from ownership of a set of skills and curricular offerings to thinking about their influence on the building and the points of entry for information, skills and lessons so that it sticks with our students and isn't relegated to just those who have the privilege of coming to the library.

For administrators, this means that we must pave the way to make changes to our curriculum and recognize that the library lessons we teach are meant to influence the entire building and not only to teach discrete skills to a specific set of students. We have to make room in librarian schedules to create space for collaboration and time for them to wield their influence on the teachers in the building.

Wielding influence means that you know what you can offer, and you make decisions based on the needs of both the program and the entire school. It also means that you must manage the changes that you introduce and understand the impact that you have on your system. Here are a few suggestions for managing that change:

- Come to your administrators with solutions, not only problems.

- Be strategic about what topics or tools you introduce to your teachers and students and when you introduce them.

- Be intentional about changes that you want to make to your program so as not to overwhelm those relying on you.

- Make student-centered decisions and support adults to implement those decisions.

- Look for opportunities to be part of conversations that will have lasting impact. Small tasks and projects are good, but what remains when the tasks are done?

#LeadingLibs Challenge

How can you build relationships and create opportunities for being a digital age mentor in your school or district? Challenge yourself with one of the activities below, and share what you're doing with the hashtag #LeadingLibs so we can all be digital age mentors for each other.

- Invite yourself to the table for a new initiative that your school or district is planning. Don't wait to be invited; take the lead in making this happen. Ask what you can help with. Ask to be on committees or the district leadership team (mission statement development, 1:1 program strategies, technology plans, curriculum writing, etc.). The more embedded you are, the more influence you wield.

- Review your school's strategic plan and identify where you might be able to offer direct support. Share your plan with your administrator using the same language found in the strategic plan, illustrating how your involvement will help meet those goals.

- Collaborate with an individual or group of teachers to identify a challenge they experience in their classroom. Brainstorm solutions that you can support as a part of the library program.

- Invite your administrators to the library to participate in the programs. Some ideas include being a guest reader for a class, volunteering at special events (e.g., the book fair, parent/child reading night, an author Skype), or teaching a tech tool they use in their work.

- Help your teachers learn a tech tool (Twitter, Instagram, etc.) that might engage the community.

- Find a mentor for yourself, and be a mentor to someone else.

Discussion Questions

1. What partnerships currently exist within the community?

2. What partnerships could you plan to cultivate?

3. What strategies can you use to build community partnerships?

CHAPTER 2

Know Your Culture

*Culture does not change because we desire to change it.
Culture changes when the organization is transformed; the
culture reflects the realities of people working together every day.*

— FRANCES HESSELBEIN, FORMER CEO OF GIRL SCOUTS
OF THE USA

When Shannon started as the librarian at Van
Meter Community School, her main goal was
to build a community within both the library
and school. A place for the students, teachers, families, and
members of the community to connect, learn, share, and be
heard. She was looking for opportunity anywhere she could
find it. In chapter 1, we discussed ways that a librarian can
build relationships, but building a community is different.
Communities are certainly about relationships, but they're
also about culture. They involve traditions, rituals, and
history. Culture drives how schools approach challenges and
opportunities, and it connects the past and present in ways

that honor where that community has been. At times, culture creates barriers to where you want to go.

We recognize that every school has their own unique community and that not every strategy and idea will work in every location. This chapter focuses on identifying and embracing the uniqueness of your individual community.

Identifying Culture

Not long ago, Bill visited a building in a Colorado a school district that was seeking help with evaluating their library program. School was in session, and the bustle of students and sound of collaboration filled the hallways. Kids were engaged and there was a vibe, just a feeling in the air, that was energizing. During a break, the librarian offered to show Bill around. As they walked, she talked about the relationships that she had with her students and teachers. She shared that this was the only building in which she had ever worked. She had started in the classroom and eventually moved into the librarian role. She was a longstanding part of the school community but was having trouble making changes to her program. "I feel like I'm in too deep," she shared. "They all trust me, but all of my teachers just want me to check out books and read to kids. I know I can do so much more, but I don't know how to get past that and to a point where I can be more beneficial to the school (Librarian)."

This conversation illustrates the conflict for many librarians. The school has a strong culture and they are successful. By all accounts, the culture of the building is a positive space where learning happens and kids are engaged. But there's also often an underlying culture that, once identified, can help our libraries make an even bigger impact on the work of the school.

The conversation shifted to the idea that there is an unspoken culture in schools, and identifying and uncovering it can be the first step toward progress in the library program. For this particular librarian, who had been embedded in this school for many years, that underlying culture was invisible until she was intentionally looking for it.

Over the next few weeks, they met through a series of video calls and tried to define her approach, and they came up with a series of questions and strategies to answer and utilize in her quest to uncover the underlying culture. Here's an abbreviated list:

- Become an impartial observer and try to see interactions as someone outside the building might.

    - How do the teachers in my building treat each other? Are there overt or underlying conflicts and resentments?

- Ask questions and listen to students.

    - What are their favorite activities or events that happen at the school?

    - Who are their school "heroes"?

- How are common areas utilized?

    - Do those in your building come together during planning periods, before or after school (or other down times)?

    - Where do most small-group meetings occur? Classrooms? Lounge? Library?

- Many schools have a climate survey. Is it possible to get the results?

These and many more questions and strategies can help to look beyond the surface of a school and get to the actual prevailing culture. For a librarian, the culture of the school is everything. Librarians must be acutely aware of their school's atmosphere and recognize its capacity for change. It's not what's evident—it's what's underlying that's important. This type of analysis is a common strategy for administrators who are looking to make changes. It can be seen as a leadership approach as well. It's hard to know how to get where you want to be if you don't know where you are.

 Librarians must be acutely aware of their school's atmosphere and recognize its capacity for change.

Being Responsive to the Community

Recognizing how a community is unique and having a keen sense of a school's atmosphere is crucial for librarians who seek to become the heart of the school. Librarians have many skills, but the most important has to do with what Eric Schenninger and Tom Murray describe as a "culture of yes" in their book, *Learning Transformed.* They suggest "you must develop a mindset for change ... [beginning with] a reflection of why change is so hard and an assessment of why previous change has failed in your school" (2017, p. 39). Due to the uniqueness of your community, there many ways to do this. Keep in mind that your school, and what goes on in it, is a reflection of the community it serves.

As a librarian, it's important to know the school and those it serves. When you seek to change culture, it's critical to know what internal and external forces are at play. You must also recognize that communities change. Each year, a new group of students joins and shapes your community. As leaders, this means that you must be flexible to identify and meet those needs while, at the exact same moment, shape the culture of the school.

Again, this is where it becomes imperative that you connect with your administrator to make sure you are on the same path. Building principals and district level leaders are constantly evaluating and considering strategies for school climate and culture. Review the strategies for building relationships that we outlined in chapter 1 to build that trust. For the librarian, make yourself an ally that is supporting the whole school. For the administrator, recognize that your librarian is one of the few people in the school that connects with every student and supports every teacher. They know the school differently than you do. Utilize their knowledge and support each other in those whole school efforts.

Plain and simple, this is hard stuff. Culture is ever-changing. However, if you are attuned to it, you can identify and even predict what's coming next. One note of caution: being responsive doesn't apply to only one area of your work. Whether you are building your collection, bringing digital tools and technology to the table, or supporting best practices in the classroom, every part of your work will constantly be in beta. It will shift from year to year, month to month, and student to student. The key is to make a habit out of observing, identifying, and responding so you are able to stay one step ahead and help to shape that culture daily, for all of your learners.

Regardless of your strategy, it's important to remember the overall goal. As Allison Zmuda and Violet Harada remind us in their book, *Librarians as Learning Specialists* (2008), "The goal is not to increase collaboration but to improve student performance" (2008, p. 31). The goal is also not to force greater participation in professional learning, create a makerspace, or have a respected program. The overall goals must remain student learning and meeting the objectives identified by the school community.

 The key is to make a habit out of observing, identifying, and responding so that you are able to stay one step ahead and help to shape that culture every day for all of your learners.

Creativity, Exploration, Discovery

Shannon often thinks about how the role of the library has changed over time, but she recognizes that, in many ways, the purpose has stayed the same. In today's classrooms, there are so many pressures on students and teachers to get through content while designing engaging learning experiences, demonstrating growth in skills and knowledge, and applying understanding to new situations. We are obviously painting with a very broad brush, and we know amazing things happen in classrooms, but one of the many things that can happen for students in libraries is the opportunity to create, explore, and discover.

It bears repeating that the experiences libraries offer outside of the classroom curriculum bolster students' creativity and help them explore the topics that interest them. In this case, it's not just about makerspaces or genius hour. Sometimes, it is helping students find just the right book, or something more advanced like 3D printing or robotics. The key here is that the library is this place. It's a place for discovery and exploration where the librarian, the library space, and the programming supports student learning and self-discovery.

An example of embracing creativity and discovery lies with Michelle Colte is a librarian at Daniel Inouya Elementary School in Wahiawa, Hawaii who brings a sense of wonder, fascination, and a love of learning to her library every single day.

LIBRARIAN PERSPECTIVE

Michelle Colte

"Would you be willing to visit my school?" This simple query has never failed me and continues to bring opportunity to my kids. I visit Geek Fests, craft fairs, and "Keiki Cons" to find makers of all types who are willing to share their creations with students. A Pokemon artist was our "artist in residence" at our Big Draw Family event, and one gentleman brought his GIANT wooden jenga, marble maze, and Connect 4 for kids to play at our Cardboard Challenge build. A local police officer and comic book artist even took the time to help our fourth graders develop comic book characters. Internally, my students can sign up to teach "lunch-time pop-ups" in the makerspace and most recently, I've invited "Maker Moms" to lead activities during recess or in conjunction with class projects. Inviting makers to make—that's my new strategy for connecting kids with information.

Take note, Michelle is not trying to be the expert or facilitate all of these experiences. Rather, she relies on her community and her network to create those opportunities. This kind of exploration and self-discovery helps her students to identify their own interests and carry that into their classroom learning experiences while at her school and as they move out of elementary education.

Figure 2.1. Students collaborating in the library.

Future Ready and ISTE Standard Connections

When we talk about developing culture, there are a number of Future Ready Librarian® framework wedges that we could be addressing (See Figure 2.2). The most obvious is the Collaborative Leadership wedge, which is the basis for much of this book. However, we would be remiss if we did not specifically point out three more.

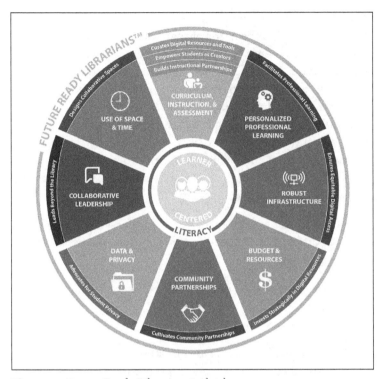

Figure 2.2. Future Ready Librarians® wheel.
Source: Alliance for Excellent Education, Future Ready Schools, and Future Ready Librarians®, reprinted with permission.

The first of these is the Personalized Professional Learning wedge. If you make a concerted effort to be an observer and listener, you will be more effective in knowing what your teaches know, and what they need to know, based on the curriculum and school goals. There are multiple entry points here, so we encourage you to rethink how you define professional learning. Just like our students, we are learning all the time, and it isn't relegated to staff meetings or trainings. If you meet with a grade-level team to help them with a new digital tool, a strategic approach to critical thinking, a lesson that includes elements of media literacy and digital citizenship, that's professional learning tailored to the needs of that particular group. Don't forget newsletters that you author, blogs you curate, or articles that you share. Each one of these activities supports culture and allows for a more robust connection between libraries and classrooms. For administrators, you already know that you have great influence over your classrooms and your teachers, but to foster cultural changes, you also have to be a coach, a supporter, a learning partner, and be in tune with the overall attitude in the building. In the new ISTE Standards for Education Leaders, this is highlighted in two places in Standard 3.

3a. Empower educators to exercise professional agency, build teacher leadership skills, and pursue personalized professional learning.

3c. Inspire a culture of innovation and collaboration that allows the time and space to explore and experiment with digital tools.

As a building leader (whether administrator or librarian), your role is to empower your teachers and sometimes that means pushing them to learn and try things outside of their comfort zone. If you're strategic and work together, you can develop the strategies that will, in time, create the culture you're looking for.

The second of the wedges we see a direct connection to is the Community Partnerships wedge. In the context of culture, we like to approach this as an opportunity to influence both our internal culture of the school as well as that of our surrounding community. Earlier, we made reference to the fact that the school is a reflection of the community. In fact, every partnership creates a tighter, more direct connection with the school, and an investment is made on both sides. These partnerships absolutely have an impact on your culture when sought and fostered. A word of caution: all community partnerships should help to meet the learning goals of the school with the spirit of making meaningful connections. Simply because an opportunity exists, does not make it the best opportunity for your school or students. There are times that partnerships might even go against the cultural shifts that you're trying to create. For example, if you partner with a vendor to bring in a reading program that tracks and directs students in their reading based on data. That could provide a big win for increasing reading levels, but it could also counteract your desire for a culture of discovery and exploration through reading, as well as tainting the relationship you have with your community when it comes to developing lifelong readers. As a leader, you have to weigh the benefits and downfalls of each partnership and enlist the help of a thinking partner to evaluate those partnerships on a strategic level. These considerations are also highlighted in the ISTE Standards for Education Leaders in standards 2 and 4.

2a. Engage education stakeholders in developing and adopting a shared vision for using technology to improve student success, informed by the learning sciences.

4d. Establish partnerships that support the strategic vision, achieve learning priorities and improve operations.

Community partnerships are critical to the success of a school's cultural health with both students and staff and can pay big dividends if intentionally harnessed and fostered.

The Curriculum, Instruction, and Assessment wedge has a strong influence on your school culture. All three edges of this particular wedge are potential culture changers, if used appropriately.

Curates Digital Resources encourages librarians to seize the opportunity to find and promote high-quality digital resources that can inspire both teachers and students to utilize the wealth of digital information and tools available to schools. The choices we make about the tools and resources that we provide to students and teachers must be intentional and deliberate. They must take into account student privacy and responsible usage and promote equitable access for students (more on this in chapter 4). This encourages administrators to recognize and actively promote digital citizenship practices and equity of access to resources that can also be found in indicator 1c in the ISTE Standards for Education Leaders, *Model digital citizenship by critically evaluating online resources, engaging in civil discourse online and using digital tools to contribute to positive social change.*

Builds Instructional Partnerships invites librarians and teachers to connect around student learning and curriculum through intentional lesson design and delivery to go beyond dissemination of information. This may mean co-teaching, coaching, or common lesson planning, but in all cases, there must be dedicated time. For administrators, we would encourage you to take a look at your schedule and the way times is allocated. Librarians can be key classroom contributors to learning, but only if they can meet with and plan with teachers. The partnership between librarian and teacher can be deep and meaningful if given time and attention, and when positively approached and celebrated, will contribute to a culture of learning and innovation in the school.

Empowers Students as Creators supports librarians' efforts to create experiences that promote discovery, collaboration, and creation both in the classroom and through library programming. We've already given some attention to this above, but it bears repeating here: When we give our students the opportunity to explore and create, we also improve our culture by offering new and exciting experiences. Indicator 3c of the ISTE Standards for Education Leaders states that leaders *inspire a culture of innovation that allows the time and space to explore and experiment with digital tools.* This connects nicely with this wedge because it provides that space for teachers to experiment, get comfortable with, and plan the implementation of digital tools in their classroom. Librarians should be seen as the conduit to bring that awareness, training, and excitement into these activities and given time to find, curate, and co-develop lessons with teachers.

These three edges, along with the Collaborative Leadership wedge, further strengthens the role librarians play in developing innovative culture that can bring about meaningful change to schools. Leaders are constantly evaluating their culture, and the partnerships that they develop with their communities are an integral piece of it. There's no single program or initiative that is going to solely change the culture of a school. Rather, it's a series of small steps moving in a combined direction that makes the cultural shift, and it will only occur if you know your culture.

#LeadingLibs Challenge

Create a culture within your library and your community that is the heart of the school. Create a place for your readers, creators, gamers, makers, writers, musicians, and all learners. The challenges for this chapter focus on making connections both in and out of your school, and they encourage you to identify and recognize your school culture and your role in its creation through flexibility, responsiveness, and leadership.

- Poll your students about their interests and personalize their experiences through a balance of books, digital tools, and experiences.

- Start a student group focused on connecting with their community and bringing positive change that they want to see in the school.

- Create a learning experience for all learners (students and adults) that allows them to be creative (maker night, STEM showcase, etc.).

- Reach out to three community leaders (government, business, etc.) inviting them to visit the school library (e.g., a special event or showcase the community leaders as the event).

- Design a space inside your library meant to cater to adults. Invite them to use it during planning time or during lunch.

- Connect a student with a book or resource that fosters social-emotional connections and helps them explore who they are.

Discussion Questions

1. How does your space promote inquiry, creativity, collaboration, and community?

2. Do you have spaces for students to create digital products documenting their learning?

3. What types of instruction do you use to promote critical thinking?

CHAPTER 3

Be a Champion

If you don't tell your story, someone else will.

— UNKNOWN

I t's clear that leadership comes in many forms. There is positional leadership that comes based on a title or a role that we play in various groups. But there's also an intangible nature to being a leader that varies depending on one's perspective and experience. Leaders don't have to be the loudest or most charismatic, but sometimes they are. Leaders also don't have to always be in charge, but they often take on that task. One thing that we feel is consistent when we consider leadership in schools is that leaders are a champion for their programs, initiatives, students, staff, and community. When we use the term "champion," what we are referring to is someone who advocates for, stands behind, and always looks out for the overall best interest of the entire picture. In our usage, "champion" is a verb and a noun. It's about the actions that one takes, the communication one gives, and who they are. Together, librarians and administrators can both "champion" for their students, staff, and programs while being a "champion" for those same groups to showcase what it means to be a citizen in the ever-changing digital age.

However, we also recognize that being a champion means that you have to know and tell your story. Before being a champion for a specific program, student, or teacher, leaders have to be strategic about what their goals are and how they are approaching those goals. You can't be a champion for everything all at once. What you can do is define your story and determine how do tell it.

One librarian that Bill has worked with, Lauren, had this realization shortly after school started one year:

> I walked into my library on an October morning, and I knew that something had to change. I was a classroom teacher and I had left the classroom two years earlier to become the librarian at the elementary school where I had taught for 10 years. My first year was all about learning about the position and researching how libraries are changing. I felt ready to take on the world, but what surprised me most about this new role was that, as a classroom teacher, my perception of what happens in the library when I dropped kids off and the actuality of what I was doing with those kids were two very different things. I hadn't really understood that being a librarian is a lot like running a small business while teaching at the same time. I had inventory, a budget, and students and adults that were looking for assistance in finding materials as well as planning for classes and other events. It was exhausting.

As time went on, she realized what many librarians have realized: teachers and administrators in her school didn't really know what she did or what she could offer. They had a view of the library based on their own, or their children's, library experiences. People understood her job as a classroom teacher. As a librarian, it was cloudier. It was time for Lauren to define and tell her story.

To get started, Bill connected her with Kim Lindskog, a library systems support specialist in his district. Kim advised her to start with data collection because, at the time, she was unable to articulate exactly what it was that she did all day. She knew she was busy helping teachers and students, but she couldn't pinpoint where all of her time went. Together, they took a three pronged approach to collecting data and discovering the library narrative.

The first data collection point was simply to use a whiteboard to provide one simple prompt for students to answer, *"I wish my library had ..."*. For two weeks she would take a picture at the end of the day before erasing what her kids had written and preparing it for the next day. She got a variety of responses including a waterslide, ice cream sandwiches, and a pet. But she also got insight through other responses like a 3D printer, more books about horses, and puzzles. Her favorite response was "I wish my library had more time for me to check out books." After two weeks she looked for themes in the answers and began to see trends in where her students' interests lie.

The second data collection point was to help her determine how she was spending her time with teachers. With people coming in and out all day, it was easy to lose track of time and lessons. In this case, Kim advised her to login to her Google Drive account and click on "Recent." At the end of each day for the same two week period, she took a screenshot of the documents that she had recently used and put that into a Google Slides presentation. Just like with the whiteboard, over the course of two weeks, she could identify the themes and the topics that were of high interest to her teachers and see what they were asking for. The story of how others saw her and what they wanted from her was beginning to come into view.

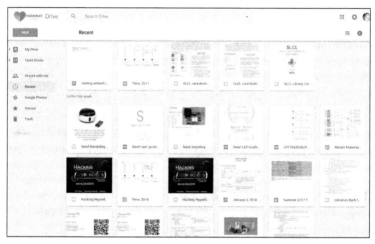

Figure 3.1. Compiled screen shots in Google Slides showing what was recently opened give insight into where time is spent.

The final data collection point is a little more formal in that Kim and Lauren created a Google Form to record the types of activities she was doing. In the form, she could indicate if the event was with a teacher, student, administrator, or parent and what type of work they were doing. She recorded duration as well as the activity. While it was difficult, she tried to record her time so that she could indicate where it was going. Using categories like library administration, collaboration, co-teaching, and professional learning communities (PLCs), she began to get insight into her daily work and was quantifying where her time went.

These three data points culminated in a narrative about the work that the library does. Even though it was initially only planned for a two week period, she continued collecting this data for another three months so that she had a broader sense of her day-to-day work. The data helped her to think beyond the frantic nature of her day and let her think about how to tell the story of her library.

As we approach what it means to advocate for your program and your library, we hope you recognize the role that collecting data plays in your work. It may not be super glamorous, but it's an important part of finding a meaningful way to tell your story.

Library Advocacy

According to the AASL Advocacy Committee, advocacy is:

> The ongoing process of building partnerships so that others will act for and with you, turning passive support into educated action for the library program. It begins with a vision and a plan for the library program that is then matched to the agenda and priorities of stakeholders.

One of the most important things we can do for our library programs (not to mention our school communities and the library profession) is to share the stories happening within our library, and show people what we do as school librarians. We must be the champions for our programs and empower others to do the same. You are the very best voice (advocate) your library has throughout your community, profession, and the world. Use that voice so your great work does not remain a highly guarded secret!

Kim Lindskog shared the following with her audience at the Missouri Association of School Librarians Conference.

> Advocacy doesn't just happen; it needs to be intentional, so making our stories visible through data provides

evidence of value and impact on student learning. Through advocacy we share library experiences about leading, teaching, and student empowerment; provide opportunities to frame what we want the users to know; and determine our priorities for not only this year, but for the future (2018).

What follows are practical examples of strategies for library advocacy. As with everything else we've discussed, not everything works everywhere. We encourage you to remember the cultural implications that we covered in chapter 2 as well as the digital mentorship approach from chapter 1. Because everything is intertwined, there is no prevailing right way.

We implore you to keep in mind the "why" behind your advocacy. When you advocate for your program, it's not about you. It's not about saving your job or the profession. It's not about showing everyone how busy you are or justifying a flexible schedule. It's about your students and the opportunities available in the library that may not be accessible in the classroom. It's about advocating for fostering creativity and curiosity in your school. It's about the love of reading and understanding what it means to be literate in the digital age. It's about the role you play in the greater school system and being a valuable piece of the educational experiences of your students. This is why you advocate, why you're a champion, and why you use your voice to shine a light on your program.

Instruction and Programming

As we look at strategies that will help you be a champion, it's important to recognize there will never be enough time to do everything that you want to do. Shannon doesn't have enough time, Bill doesn't have enough time, and neither do you. You have to prioritize and figure out what decisions you can make that will best meet the goals of your school and your program. If something doesn't align with one of those sets of goals, you need to strongly consider whether to pursue it.

Here's the thing: you will have to say "no" to good things. You have to be strategic about what you say "yes" to. Focus on outcomes as opposed to tasks, and be sure that you recognize and understand the implications of both "yes" and "no." Remember that we're all busy. Just because you have a busy calendar doesn't mean that you're being effective. It means you're doing lots of stuff.

 Just because you have a busy calendar doesn't mean that you're being effective. It means you're doing lots of stuff.

So what does that mean for your curriculum and instruction, and how does one advocate through curriculum? In chapter 2 we briefly addressed curriculum through creativity, exploration, and discovery. In Bill's district, they look at the library curriculum as the curriculum of the entire school district. Nothing is taught in isolation, and everything should connect in some way to the classroom. They try to fill in the gaps of the overall student learning experience and work collaboratively to balance the core curriculum with exploring a wide variety of topics to help students find their personal interests through the activities and content with which they connect them. If we are to lead, we cannot see ourselves on an island of instruction or programming. Connections must be made.

You are Educators

In modern school libraries, a variety of roles support learning, and the contributions that all of these individuals make should not be overlooked or discounted. In our schools, libraries are an integral part of the educational programming for the students you serve. You bring expertise in curation, research, digital tools, and content, to name a few. Similar to Lauren when she was in the classroom, there are those in your school community who may think that your job entails reading to students, shelving and checking out books, and doing arts and crafts as a part of a makerspace. If you don't tell them differently, that's the story they tell themselves, their students, and their families. You are educators but your students are many, and they each have their own needs when it comes to your role. Consider the following strategies for bringing your library to the world:

- Send a short weekly or daily email to teachers, highlighting the work their students did in the library that week, naming the goals that it works toward, and how it will help their students.

- Invite teachers and administrators to sit in on your lessons.

- Send summary emails home with students.

- Video students talking about what they are learning.

- Highlight student work in the library.

As with everything you do, keeping students at the center of the story that you tell has a stronger impact than focusing on tasks you have completed.

For administrators, you also have a role in telling the story of the library. That could mean highlighting the activities that go on in the library, providing funding for materials, furniture or programming, or even something as simple as providing the time and venue (faculty or parent meeting) to put the librarian in a position of leadership to share the great things to staff or parents. More than anything, if your librarian hasn't defined their story, push them to be able to articulate the value they bring and the experiences of the students they serve. Use this book to showcase what a library could look like and how to lead through the library to serve the school community.

Programming

To be a champion, you must be intentional about the topics you cover in your instruction and the opportunities you create for your learners. We are more convinced than ever that the library curriculum is not relegated to the library. Certainly there are skills which are library specific, but when we consider curriculum as a whole, and the goals that we seek to accomplish, the library curriculum is a piece of the bigger picture. For instance, research is a major skill taught in libraries. Research for the sake of research is not the goal. Rather, we want students who can use their research skills in the classroom as needed. This seems obvious, but too many library curriculums are intended to stand alone. It's important to see beyond what happens when students are inside the walls of your library and recognize that the entire curriculum a student experiences is also your curriculum. Libraries support learning in all forms while nurturing a spirit of discovery and exploration.

If we consider the guiding documents that we referenced for school libraries, it's clear that we can't meet our library goals without looking at the entire student experience. When we think about programming and curriculum in that broader sense, these documents become more relevant, and referencing them helps us to tell our stories.

We encourage you to pause for a moment and take a look at the documents in Figure 3.2.

Figure 3.2. Guiding documents for school libraries.

Where in these documents can you identify opportunities to tell your story and highlight the work your students are doing? Consider that, in the AASL Standards, the foundations and the domains competencies are not library specific. The ISTE Standards focus on what we want students to be instead of what we want them to do. In the Future Ready Librarians® Framework, there is a distinct commitment to supporting the work of the entire district over teaching discrete skills.

This doesn't mean that you throw out your lessons or discard your state or district standards. However, it does beg us to recognize that all lessons should be working toward an overall goal, and that's not something you can do alone. This might mean that it's not as important that students learn these specific skills in the library. What's important is that they learn the skills.

Telling Your Story Through Programming

As we've discussed in previous chapters, being responsive to the needs of your community is vital, and every decision you make with your programming and your content should be intentional. Here are some strategies to consider:

Promote the ISTE Standards. When you are collaborating with teachers, look for opportunities to include language from the ISTE Standards, and focus on what it looks like for students to be an empowered learner, digital citizen, and so on. Introducing this language in those conversations, and naming how you support students in that endeavor, can help tremendously. We've even seen librarians label their lessons with ISTE Standards and use the language with students, too.

Collaborate. As you work with teachers, recognize that collaboration is a two-way street; it is not simply your job to support what teachers want to do. Your goals are part of the equation as well, and these are opportunities to talk with teachers about the work you've done in other classes, in the hopes of fueling ideas and new thinking. If your school utilizes PLCs, make an effort to be part of the planning and implementation. Bring your expertise and perspective to the conversations.

Advertise. Sometimes Shannon thinks of herself as the cruise director for her school. She organizes initiatives, connects teachers, leads professional learning, and her teachers feel like they can always come to her for answers. But this reputation doesn't just happen. Over the years, Shannon proved herself to be resourceful and helpful but it goes beyond that. One of the best things she did for her program was to start blogging (**vanmeterlibrary voice. blogspot.com**). This online space gave her an opportunity to tell her story by highlighting what students were doing, and what connections they were making. By sharing it with her staff, Shannon gave them a window into what students were learning and advertised the programming in her library.

Connect. Don't forget to connect the work that your students do and the programming that you design to the overall goals of the school. If your school is focused on character education, how can you help teach students about empathy through literature? If there are reading goals, what can you do to support them? Regardless of the goal, find the data points that support the programming you're providing and showcase that data. Help to lead that work while also supporting it.

When it comes to programming, your actions—and the activities that you plan—speak louder than anything that you might say. Promote the work that learners do, whether adults or students, and make it clear that they are working toward bigger things beyond what are regarded as traditional library goals.

Amplifying Student Voice

Another great opportunity to be a champion in the library is to amplify the voices of your students. As an administrator, Bill often looked at the landscape of schools very holistically. He knows that many nuances and dynamics are invisible to him, but he loves to walk into buildings and see students who are sharing their voices in a variety of ways. Sometimes it's daily video announcement broadcasts, and other times it's displays of student work. In all cases, it's apparent that there is a culture that celebrates students.

Librarians and libraries are in a unique position to foster and build relationships with students. Like few other places in the school community, we have the chance to get to know all of the students within our building every year. We get to learn what they are passionate about and have chances to listen, to encourage, to support, and most of all, to be the champion all students need. We can give them the chance to be heard, but we have to recognize the opportunities as they arise and take advantage of them.

The abundance of free digital tools makes amplifying student voices more possible than ever. However, it's important to think about how this will play out in reality. Student voices can be heard in a variety of ways and, in all actuality, our students don't need us to use their voices. They have the tools available to them now. They are already creators and producers at all grade levels. Depending on their ages, the students in your building may already have YouTube channels or other avenues where they share videos they have created, while others may have podcasts or stream their video games on Twitch (a video game streaming platform). For those students, we must honor their voices and not suggest that video games don't have value. As of February 2018, Twitch had over 2.2 million unique monthly broadcasters and 355 billion minutes watched (Perez, 2018). School isn't the only place where values are created. Hobbies and interests that aren't valued in school are often highly valued in other areas of the community.

For libraries, this is a way to showcase the work that our students are doing and celebrate their movement toward the goals of students meeting the ISTE Standards (and others) already discussed. By tying digital creation and student voice to library lessons, we can have our students create public service announcement videos about search techniques or a bank of screencast tutorials showing their classmates how to use a specific tool. We can stream or record classroom presentations and share them beyond the classroom or create posters that draw attention to a character education initiative or future school event.

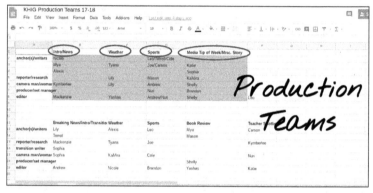

Figure 3.3. Student production team spreadsheet identifying student jobs for their newscast.

One example of engaging students in digital creation and student voice can be seen at Highcroft Ridge Elementary in Chesterfield, Missouri where librarian Danielle Stilts engages her students in digital creation through the use of digital tools by creating an opportunity for her students to create a student-led newscast based on stories that are important to them. Each student takes on a role in the production process and, after doing the research, writing the script, and recording and editing the video, their creation is broadcast throughout the school. "It's been great for them to experience the creation process in a way that they don't have time to in their classrooms," Danielle says. "The investment in the work is off the charts, and they love to celebrate their final project with the rest of the school." She is also proud of the collaboration and teamwork that they display as they work through technical issues and "creative disagreements" while still focusing on the craft of putting together a story for others.

Truly, the possibilities are endless. While some of your students will need help with how to use these tools, many won't. In those cases, your role is to amplify and draw attention to the end results. Act as a consultant for how and what students are communicating and the most effective way to do that. Give your students choice in both the products and the processes as they are creating. Whether student work happens in the library, the classroom, or outside of school, celebrate and showcase that work and amplify the voices of your students.

Connecting to the Community

We are past the days where the library is a single place and where your influence is relegated to people in the library space. Many of the libraries we work with are getting outside of their buildings and making significant impacts on their local communities as well as the global landscape. Kristen Mattson, school library director at Waubonsie Valley High School in Aurora, Illinois, is a Future Ready Librarian® and author of *Digital Citizenship in Action: Empowering Students to Engage in Online Communities* (2017). During her tenure, she has made significant strides in bringing her work to the greater community.

Kristen's approach has helped her to reach out and be responsive to the needs of her community. In today's world, the library is no longer merely a physical space, and the digital components and catalog are just as important as the books and furniture found in the actual building.

LIBRARIAN PERSPECTIVE

Kristen Mattson

As the only librarian in a high school that serves 2,600 students, I often find myself needing to be in more than one place at a time. A teacher may ask for a research mini-lesson on the same day that I am already working with a class on a new technology tool. My saving grace in this situation was my thoughtfully designed web presence. When developing my library site, I opted for a sleek design with limited text, beautiful pictures, and embedded videos that would appeal to my high school audience. Over the last four years I've created dozens of videos on everything from how to navigate academic databases to engaging book trailers and ways to troubleshoot a Chromebook. These videos help teachers reinforce lessons I've given earlier in the year, allow students to take library instruction home with them, and have allowed me to duplicate my efforts and influence—expanding my reach in such a large school.

Opportunities abound for connecting with the community through your library. One of the easiest ways to get involved locally is through a partnership with the public library. You may have different missions and reach, but you share patrons and can support each other's work by connecting and promoting the programming in both spaces. Following are some ideas for connecting with the community.

- Provide students with public library cards to eliminate barriers to accessing resources.

- Promote summer and school reading programs.

- Offer professional learning to school librarians about databases and resources available through the public library.

- Investigate public programs. Some public libraries have programs that will come to schools and do different activities (STEM, makerspace, etc.) with students.

As you are making connections in your community, don't forget the global community. There is more evidence than ever that we are in a global economy; we all influence each other's work. That greater library community is more accessible than ever.

Jennifer Casa-Todd is a teacher-librarian in the York Catholic District School Board in Aurora, Ontario, Canada and sees herself as a global connector for her school and, through these global projects, she is able to connect her work to that of her teachers and form a bond that goes beyond an individual project.

 ## LIBRARIAN PERSPECTIVE

Jennifer Casa-Todd

Over the course of a year, I seek out several global projects for us to participate in so that my students can connect with others around the world. I do the initial work of getting the information and logistics figured out, and then I invite my teachers to join in full partnership with me. For the past two years we have participated in a global project, #BeTheChangeTakeTheChallenge organized by a teacher in Norway and focused on the UN Sustainable Development Goals. Through projects like this one, I have been able to support teachers not just to use tools to connect (Webroom, Flipgrid, Twitter) when they may not be comfortable, but together we collaborate and take risks to create engaging learning experiences for our students.

Stories like Jennifer's show the power of connecting beyond your library are plentiful in the online communities that have formed in recent years. As of this writing, the Future Ready Librarians® Facebook group has right at 20,000 members from all over the world, and there are Twitter chats for librarians that occur on an almost daily basis. The ISTE Librarian Professional Learning Network is one of the most active of the ISTE PLN communities and companies like Follett are creating their own online spaces for librarians to connect and share their work.

 When it comes to a digital presence, it's not important that you're everywhere; it's important that you're somewhere.

Online spaces are not the only place to connect with others and your community. Look for local networking groups, library or tech conferences, Edcamps, or other face-to-face meetings. When you attend, put yourself out there and think about each person you meet as an opportunity to learn something. We know that it may be uncomfortable, but Bill regularly tells people about a conversation that he had with Joseph South, ISTE's Chief Learning Officer, where he talked about a strategy that he had used to break the ice in a social setting: "Just ask them what they're excited about." That opening is all many people need to begin a conversation because everyone is excited about something. In Bill's experience, this one phrase provides the invitation to not just make small talk, but to create connections between the two of you whatever the topic. They key though is that, once the question is asked, it's important to listen to the answer and look for connections to keep the conversation going.

As you can see, the bar is low for connecting beyond your school library because of the technology that is available to us, however, we also know that it can be overwhelming because there are so many tools and options that it's hard to choose which one. When it comes to a digital presence, it's not important that you're everywhere; it's important that you're somewhere. Find the community that is going to work for you, and take that first step. If you're already a Twitter user, do a search for #TLChat and see what people are posting. Share a link or an idea of your own. Everyone has something to offer. It's just a matter of finding what that something is for you. Wherever you land, just remember that in every community, the more you contribute, the more you will get out of it. Resources abound, let's help each other find our way through this digital age!

Table 3.1 | Some of Our Favorite Resources

Future Ready Librarians® Facebook group	Facebook.com/groups/ futurereadylibrarians	
TLChat	twitter.com/TLChat	
ISTE Librarians PLN	librariansnetwork.weebly.com	

Continued

#FutureReadyLibs	twitter.com/hashtag/futurereadylibs	
Follett Project Connect case studies	www2.follettlearning.com/projectconnect	
Alliance of Excellence Education Future Ready Librarians® webinars	all4ed.org/webinars-events	
ISTE Librarian resources	iste.org/librarians	
ISTE Standards and Future Ready Librarians® Crosswalk	iste.org/learn/librarians	
ISTE U Future Ready Librarians® course	iste.org/learn/iste-u/library-practices	
AASL Resources	ala.org/aasl	

#LeadingLibs Challenge

To be a champion for your program and your students, you must be your own advocate. In these challenges, we encourage you to identify and share your story. Be creative! Look for others who have a voice in the community and encourage them to share the library's impact on their lives. Your voice is powerful; find it and use it. Don't forget to share your story online and tag it with #LeadingLibs.

- Create a plan for branding your library and telling your story. We recommend thinking in both the short term (3–6 months) and long term (3–5 years). Remember that you will always be in beta and your plan will change. Write it down so you can refer to it.

- Start a blog or publish a newsletter (paper or online with Google Slides or Smore). Use this to highlight student work, inform and promote your programming, advertise new books, and for professional learning for your community. Push it through email and social media to connect with local and global communities.

- Study the ISTE Standards so you can use the language as a part of your collaborative conversations. Initially, you don't have to mention them as standards (it may be overwhelming to add another set of standards), but use the language so your colleagues become familiar with it. If they want to know more, point them in that direction.

    - *Stage 2 Challenge:* Introduce the ISTE Standards to your staff when you think they are ready and ask for time in a faculty meeting to offer development around them. Discuss them as indicators of what we want our students to BE rather than DO.

- Create a student advisory group that is charged with finding opportunities to amplify student voice, and honor what is created both in and out of school.

- Explore the resources and community offers available from your local public library. Connect and offer to partner with them to expand programming opportunities for your students.

Discussion Questions

1. What are examples of communication tools we could use with parents that encourage engagement in the student learning process?

2. What do you want teachers, students, parents, and administrators to say about your library?

3. How can you lead and advocate for your program without making it seem self-serving?

CHAPTER 4

Leading
Through Equity

Not everything that is faced can be changed.
But nothing can be changed until it is faced.

— JAMES BALDWIN

B ill remembers being a student worker in his college
library, listening to the library staff talking about
ways for students to have more equitable access to
information. This was before the internet was readily accessible in dorms, and smartphones were still many years from
coming to market. The library staff had expressed frustra-
tion with not only the finite supply of resources (databases
and books) they could physically house and manage, but
also with the fact that they were unable to reach more
students in their small college. They lamented that there
were only a handful of professors who asked for their help
with research instruction and that they were often seen as
"collectors of books" rather than curators of information.

Twenty years later, Bill is responsible for the library program in his district, and he often has the very same conversation with the librarians he works with. While some of the mediums have changed, and access to information is greater than it's ever been, we still discuss the equity gap we see in our schools.

For the purposes of this book, we are going to focus on equity in two very narrow ways: equity of experience and equity of digital content. We recognize that there are huge access gaps across the U.S., not to mention the rest of the world. Whether these gaps involve access to technology and devices or access to a reliable internet connection, these are problems that we continue to address throughout our schools. However, we are relieved that there are individuals, organizations, and companies working tirelessly to address equity gaps and bring awareness and connectivity to schools and communities. There is still a long way to go before we are able to say that access is truly equitable, but, through programs like E-Rate, strides are being made. We aren't specifically addressing those topics in this chapter, but that doesn't let us off the hook. Libraries and librarians should see themselves as leaders in this work and be constant voices advocating for equity of devices and internet access for all of our students and families. If, for some reason, this is not a topic of conversation in your community, we encourage you to start it and begin to close those gaps locally.

Equity of Experience

In 2016, a new draft of the National Educational Technology Plan was introduced from the U.S. Office of Educational Technology. In that document, one of the topics that helped to shape our thinking about equity was that of equity of experience. When we think about our students entering their classrooms, we know they will have very different experiences using technology based on the interests of individual classroom teachers. In some cases, classrooms are completely void of technology and reliance on information outside of the textbook. In other cases, we see rich, authentic learning experiences that utilize technology in meaningful ways and engage students in learning activities that utilize the power of the vast information available. As you might have gathered, we prefer the second classroom.

When we focus on equity of experience, we focus on the decisions we make as educators and the invitations we extend to learn and interact with different types of content. Libraries are unique in that we can offer experiences that extend the classroom and are not bound to the same type of curricular constraints. We can focus on what it means to be literate in the digital age, and we can help students explore their interests. At the same time, we can lead our schools by providing models for innovative instruction and resources while supporting classrooms. Equity of experience doesn't mean that all classrooms have identical experiences. Rather, it's a focus on recognizing the time in which we live and utilizing the tools of the day. It's no longer acceptable for technology usage to be an option based on adult interests or comfort levels.

Focusing on Literacy

As we stated previously, we know that being literate in the digital age is different than it once was. It requires a different set of skills and dispositions to be able to navigate the digital world and consider ourselves knowledgeable and successful in that navigation. What's interesting is that we also apply the word "literacy" to many different areas of study. We have media literacy, digital literacy, transliteracy, technology literacy, and many others that classify the thinking and skills needed to navigate different facets of the world. While it's convenient to label different topics as their own literacy, we feel that, when all is said and done, all of these topics come together and define what it means to be literate in today's world. Can one be "literate" in the digital age without having an understanding of the messages of media or how to critically consume information? We would argue that they cannot, and the same holds true many, if not all, of the "literacies" that we continue to define and subcategorize. We are not condemning these different labels. We recognize that sometime it can help define and explain a concept and give some common language. In this instance, we are just suggesting that all these "literacies" overlap and inform each other to create a truly literate person.

When we consider literacy through the lens of library programs and equity of experience, there are a few topics that we simply must explore and, as we addressed in chapter 1, to become digital age mentors for all members of our greater school community. Those topics are:

- Critical consumption of information

- Media

- Research

- Technology

- Digital citizenship

As school leaders, each of these topics brings with it a great many challenges and opportunities, but each should be addressed in its own right. If we intend to help students become members of a society that is driven, in many cases, by technology and digital content, these are critical skills that can help students throughout their lives and are far more important than an individual fact that we might assess them on for a single unit or lesson. While this list is not comprehensive, it does represent a starting point for considering topics that will move your program beyond traditional definitions of literacy.

Critical Consumption of Information

As we look at trends in news coverage, bias, and how we share and personally vet information, being critical consumers of information is one of the most important skills that we can teach our students. We must teach them to question everything and seek to understand the views and values of others. Librarians are, once again, in a unique position to help bring structure and strategies to utilizing and verifying the information we find. These skills include finding the most trustworthy sources, a willingness to seek multiple perspectives on a subject, and developing one's own opinions based on reliable information. As time goes on, these skills will become a differentiator for students and adults alike, and they are a critical issue when discussing equity.

Media

Media and information literacy are similar in approach, but for our purposes, we are going to focus on the need to understand, verify, and utilize the messages that we get from the various forms of media with which we interact. Regardless of your opinion about today's media, it's clear we live in a very visual world. Images and video have become even more prevalent through digital tools, so we must help our students understand the messages that they are both consuming and creating. When photos can easily be altered and video can be quickly edited, we must have a healthy sense of skepticism; what we see is not always to be believed. As with information, we must take the time to verify and actively seek out truth with a deeply developed understanding of media messages and the hidden purposes with which they are created. In this instance, it's as important to ask what we are not seeing or hearing as what we are.

Research

It is becoming more and more obvious that the definition of research in our schools needs to change. Traditionally, students and teachers view research as an event, a project or task that has a beginning and an end. In these cases, a product is created, and it signifies that research is complete. However, because of the rise of information and digital tools, we all do research every day. Maybe we look up something simple, such as a conversion table for units of measure or a tutorial on a task we are trying to complete, or maybe it's something as complex as the vastness of the universe. Either way, research is closely tied to information and media as a piece of the literacy puzzle. Research continues to shift with advances in technology, and it's important that we question and analyze our results. In today's world, we can ask voice assistants for answers to questions, but how do we know they're right? How do we verify our answers, ask meaningful questions, and have the stamina to find the right answer in a variety of situations? When do we seek more information, and when are we confident in a quick result? Redefining research is one of the many parts of the quest to find and address equity in our schools and communities.

Technology

Over the last ten years, the rapid advances in technology, and how it has influenced our lives, is astounding—and there's no indication that it will slow down. Therefore, what it means to be literate in the digital age must include an understanding of how to utilize technology in meaningful ways and be familiar with the various available tools so we are able to choose the appropriate tool for a specific task. It doesn't stop there. We must also be able to reflect on the role technology plays in our lives and explore the implications of our decisions. This might include ethical dilemmas regarding how the technology we create might be used (weaponry, for instance), as well as our health and well-being as users of technology. Self-regulation and learning to control our usage will continue to be important skills as more digital tools are embedded in our lives. While technology will become less expensive and more accessible, conversations around equity will live in these skills.

Digital Citizenship

We tend to view digital citizenship and digital literacy in the same way. By putting the word *digital* in front of *citizenship*, it somehow qualifies citizenship as something that happens only in digital spaces and is only relevant to technology. However, we like to think about it as "citizenship in the digital age," making it a more mainstream conversation for which everyone in a school community is responsible. That said, this is still an opportunity for librarians to provide leadership and address equity gaps. Again, this is another instance where you need to fully understand the culture of your school and community. We recommend tying digital conversations to any character education initiatives that might be happening in your school to make discrete connections for all involved.

It is our hope that these important topics are already resonating with you and that maybe you already have initiatives in place to help your community understand the need for such a focus. Much like with more traditional literacy initiatives, addressing each of these topics is not the role of a single person, but rather must be a team effort. Once again, librarians and administrators can take this opportunity to partner and problem solve together.

In the digital age, these topics are the realm of the librarian. While you need not have all the answers, it's important to have a working knowledge and familiarity of the concepts, hot topics, and resources that are available to schools. As we said above, research may seem obvious and is often where librarian expertise lies, but each of the previous topics are part of our digital landscape and should be treated with the same diligence as we use when building our catalog of books.

For administrators, it's sometimes easy to get bogged down in the day-to-day of running a building or working in a district. However, these topics are of great importance to the school and community climate and to the futures of those in our care. While priorities must be made, it's becoming more and more clear that the combination of technology and literacy cannot simply be an add-on or an afterthought. It must be part of a concerted and combined effort to help students make good decisions around their use of technology.

Recently, Bill had a conversation with a group of administrators at a workshop around their character education initiatives in their buildings. Each leader was talking about how they were approaching helping their students be caring and considerate of each other, and how they hope to instill confidence in their lives while teaching them to do the right thing. Throughout the entire conversation, no mention was made of digital tools or online behavior in connection to character education. As the conversation was winding down, Bill inquired about where they think technology fits in. "If they know how to treat each other face-to-face, they can do it online too," was one of the answers he got. While technically, this may be true, in reality, we recognize that there is a perception of anonymity when online. We regularly hear stories of students, and adults, posting things online that they would never actually say in public. This contradiction is rampant and widely seen as hypocritical in the eyes of our students. Through ongoing, targeted education that addresses our online interactions and focuses on what to do as opposed to what not to do, we can begin to have meaningful conversations about the role of digital spaces in our character education.

Equity of Digital Content

When it comes to equity, the second lens that we want to consider is that of digital content and access for students. Classroom content continues to evolve; it is becoming more dynamic, relevant, and accessible for our students. However, as this evolution occurs, it also means that we must somehow wrangle it into easily accessible and usable formats. From the administrator lens, this means that we must either set or advocate for policies that demand that our purchases and subscriptions can be used by all who need it. In Bill's district, he has recently been leading his curriculum department through considerations that must be made when adopting digital resources and developing an ongoing plan to ensure that when resources are adopted, there is consideration as to if and how digital content fits into the adoption. They still have plenty of books and physical materials, but, in the long run, he sees those adoptions moving to a "digital first" strategy where digital materials take priority and physical materials are supplemental, rather than the other way around. This, along with guaranteed access to devices, gives greater flexibility, searchability, and scalability to the content.

For Ashley Cooksey, library media specialist at Batesville School District in Batesville, Arkansas, one of her approaches to providing access to digital content is through a partnership she has fostered with her local county library.

LIBRARIAN PERSPECTIVE

Ashley Cooksey

This year our school is 1:1, 24/7/365 for Grades 6–12 which brings a need for access to digital content. I have been able to partner with our local county library to provide all students in Grades 6–12 with an e-book library allowing our students to access thousands of e-books and audio books free of charge! Our public county library is part of a state consortium that allows patrons to use inter-library loan for digital materials, and since they're digital, there are no late fees for students to worry about. To serve the needs of all in my community, we have decided to present our parents with an option to opt-out of the program if they do not want their student to have a digital library card.

Many school libraries are beginning to take this route to provide students with the access they already have but to simplify the process so that it can be part of the school enrollment. This removes one more barrier for students to get the information they need.

As librarians, it's even more important to understand the intricacies of how all the tools work together. For instance, Google's G Suite and Chromebooks have become increasingly popular due to their collaborative nature, ease of management, and lower cost. As a district or school moves to adopt these types of tools, someone (we'd recommend a librarian) needs to point out the changes that must take place in adult behavior for such initiatives to be effective. One of those changes involves digital content and how it's delivered to students. While there are tips, tricks, and tools to get around it, interoperability of documents and files becomes more important. For instance, if students primarily use Chromebooks in their classrooms, the only software we can guarantee students have access to is Google Drive. If teachers are posting or sharing documents in another format (Word, PowerPoint, Excel, etc.), those files must be converted by students. It seems simple, but why would we create barriers to entry for students when this could be identified early? In this case, librarians might provide development for teachers about how to effectively convert or compose in the corresponding Google tool. The platform (Google, Apple, Microsoft) is less important than the concept. There are lots of opinions when it comes to which tool to use, but we have to look beyond a platform or tool and work with whatever tool comes with our learners.

Access to information is one of our top priorities when we lead through equity. This concept extends to databases, digital textbooks, ebooks, and so on. Learning can happen anywhere, at any time, and it's incumbent upon us to be sure that the resources we provide can be accessed outside of school hours and the school building.

The final element of digital content involves the types of experiences that we regularly offer our students. Throughout both their schooling and their lives, they will experience content in a variety of different mediums. We have been, and continue to be, in a time of transition when it comes to texts. For instance, it's no longer acceptable for us to invite students to use only one medium to read. They need multiple experiences with different types of mediums so they have the skills to effectively interact with these different types of texts. We still need to help them recognize text features in books and understand how they function, but it's equally important to help students understand hyperlinks, the connected web, and features that occur in online spaces. They need skills in building stamina for reading chapter books, but they also need a different kind of stamina to bypass the multitude of ads on a website and focus on the content. They need experience "reading" YouTube videos and interactive infographics as much as they need to read graphs in a textbook. Once again, this is an area in which librarians can lead their colleagues to be intentional about how students interact with different texts and the skills they need in each medium.

Both of these topics are directly addressed in the Future Ready Librarians® Framework through the Robust Infrastructure, Budget, and Resources wedges. There are countless strategies that can be leveraged here, but the important piece is that you are paying attention, engaging in the conversation, and advocating for students every step of the way. Of equal importance is that you understand your school culture and recognize how change-tolerant your system is. You are partly responsible for that culture and, while it may take time, patience is also an effective strategy. If you advocate for students and get a "no," recognize that you are just one step closer to "yes" because you know what isn't an option. Lead through the change and pave the way by setting the expectation that all of your digital resources are accessible by all students. Hold your content providers to that same standard. Don't forget that these are all opportunities to form partnerships between building and district leaders and librarians in order to make a difference. In some cases, the equity issues that we see are systemic to the policies and procedures in a school. Addressing these issues takes a willingness to identify issues, the courage to address them, and a strategic approach to solving them.

Connecting to the Standards

Equity is one of those topics that continue to grow and change as technology becomes more a part of our schools and our instruction. This is one of the many reasons that we find the ISTE Standards to be so valuable for the work happening in schools. The topic of equity can be referenced many times throughout ISTE's collection of standards but we want to take a moment to make some direct connections to the Standards for Educational Leaders and expand on how the language and spirit with which they were written can be valuable as you address the equity issues you may find in your system.

STANDARD 1. EQUITY AND CITIZENSHIP ADVOCATE

INDICATOR 1.A

Ensure all students have skilled teachers who actively use technology to meet student learning needs.

This indicator speaks to equity of experience for students in the classroom. Librarians and administrators can help address this equity issue by providing the necessary instructional support in the use of technology so that teachers are prepared to meet the needs of their students. This could be a series of trainings, encouraging just-in-time professional development, or introducing and maintaining high quality digital tools and content to be used in the classroom.

INDICATOR 1.B

Ensure all students have access to the technology and connectivity necessary to participate in authentic and engaging learning opportunities.

Ensuring that all students have access is not a trivial task, but it is one that's well worth the effort. This may require a policy change or creative thinking when it comes to spending, but schools all over the country are tackling this in different ways. From equipping busses with wifi, negotiating rates for housing complexes for affordable internet service, exploring broadband wifi or partnering with local businesses and communities to welcome students to use an internet connection, there are many ways to get access into the community. By the same token, there are companies who will donate computers to schools for use by students and families while some schools extend their hours and provide computer use to families after hours. Creativity and working together can go a long way when trying to address student needs.

INDICATOR 1.C

Model digital citizenship by critically evaluating online resources, engaging in civil discourse online and using digital tools to contribute to positive social change.

We've already discussed both digital citizenship and evaluating online tools in previous sections of this chapter, but the last part of this indicator stands out to us because of the weight that it carries. As educators we know we are role models when our students see us on a daily basis, but that modeling can go far beyond the classroom and extend into our personal, digital lives. It's important that our students see those they know engaging in online discourse in a civilized manner. Through modeling and our consistent approach in how we engage others in digital spaces, we can battle the perception of toxicity that we find in many online social networks. To that end, we can also make important contributions to society and create social change, but only if we monitor our online presence and contribute positively in a way that our students can see us.

STANDARD 2. VISIONARY PLANNER

INDICATOR 2.B

Build on the shared vision by collaboratively creating a strategic plan that articulates how technology will be used to enhance learning.

We look at this indicator as directly relating back to the concept of equity of experience. Only by working together to create a plan can we influence how technology is used in the classroom and the ways in which we develop the skill set of our teachers to be able to not just teach *with* technology, but to *utilize* technology to engage students in meaningful work. We should not use technology for the sake of using it, but instead think of it as the vehicle in which learning can occur.

STANDARD 4. SYSTEMS DESIGNER

INDICATOR 4.C

Protect privacy and security by ensuring that students and staff observe effective privacy and data management policies.

This last standard and indicator references back to the digital content that we bring into our schools for our students to use. Whether through policy or through practice, we must determine best practices to protect our students' privacy. It's more than just a compliance with federal and/or state legislation. We would argue that it's our moral duty to ensure the privacy of our students as they learn how to explore the digital world in a space where we can help them make mistakes and learn how to manage the online world. One word of warning though, it's not enough to simply protect them. It's imperative that we have regular, ongoing conversations about how to protect our own privacy and security, otherwise we run the risk of protecting them so much that they don't know what to do when they are not sitting in front of us or on our filtered network.

As you can see, equity encompasses many facets of our schools and is one of the topics that we must continue to bring to the forefront as both administrators and librarians. As leaders, in your respective spaces, your influence can make significant changes to your systems for the betterment of all you serve.

#LeadingLibs Challenge

We expect to struggle with equity for many years. For our purposes, we know we did not do it justice. Our challenge to you is to create a sense of urgency around bringing equitable access to your students. The following list can get you started but, as you strive to lead from the library, be a voice for your students and make equity a priority. Don't forget to share your stories using the #LeadingLibs tag so we can all learn together.

- Seek an opportunity to ask questions about equity in your school community. Bring up equity of experience or equity of digital content in that conversation.

- Host a literacy night that includes digital topics, and talk about what it means to be literate in the digital age.

- Develop a plan for helping teachers have ongoing conversations about their digital lives and the decisions they make when using digital tools.

- Audit the digital content you provide your students. Do your students have access outside of your building and school hours? If not, develop a plan to address this.

- Review the National Educational Technology Plan, referencing opportunities to create more equitable opportunities for your students.

- Begin (or continue) the conversation about developing a digital content strategy meant to help define potential student privacy concerns.

- Ask your administrator to lead a part of professional development coming up within your building or district. If this is already how you lead, perhaps you are ready to expand your leadership. Ask for the first 10 minutes of every meeting to share, teach, and lead learning. Discuss the impact this has on your library program and the teachers' practice with your administrator.

Discussion Questions

1. How do you support district goals such as equity of experiences, access to resources, and empowering creativity?

2. Do the materials you curate create roadblocks or pathways when considered through the lens of equity?

3. What might a digital content strategy look like in order to address the acquisition of digital resources and tools?

CHAPTER 5

A Force for Change

The world as we have created it is a process of our thinking.
It cannot be changed without changing our thinking.

—ALBERT EINSTEIN

hroughout the pages of this book, we have discussed how one might lead through a library program. We'd like to end by encouraging you to examine the ways in which you and your programs can be a force for change in your schools. We hear from school librarians who don't feel valued and are concerned about the future. We hear about programs being cut, leaving students with missed opportunities for connections and the exploration of their personal interests. We also hear about amazing programs with Future Ready Librarians® who are making a difference in the lives of students.

Wherever your program is, and whatever the climate of your state or school community, the world needs you. The world needs librarians. We need you to be the voice of the students in your community. We need you to know your school better than anyone else. We need you to be digital mentors who share your stories and advocate for equity in our schools. Above all, we need you to continue working hard to bring about change and relevance in our schools. We know this is a tall order, but we also recognize that you are librarians—this is what you do.

Making A Difference

Don't overthink your role as a leader. Yes, leadership is strategic, but it also requires action. It requires you to think beyond your program and find ways to make a difference. Sometimes getting started is the hardest part. We want to think, plan, and make sure we're right. Unfortunately, you don't have time. You owe it to every learner with whom you interact to get started today. Don't worry. You can do this.

Part of making a difference is making your program matter to others. At one point, libraries mattered largely because of the information and resources they housed. As information becomes more accessible, the reason libraries matter must change. In school libraries, make your program relevant by connecting the work, language, and collaborations to other district, school, and community initiatives. If coding and computer science are important to your school, offering extension activities to the curriculum supports everyone while connecting computer science directly to the library. Use Hour of Code (**hourofcode.com**) to help kids go deeper in their coding experience or utilize free club programs like CS First (**csfirst.withgoogle.com**) from Google. If that's not what will make the difference, go a different direction. The key is that you must go. You must take action to make a difference.

At this point you may be thinking, "action ... yeah, that's cool and all but how do I actually do this?" The answer is ... It depends. It depends on what's important to you and what's important to your community. It depends on what you've done so far and what you want to do next. It depends on many, many things. But, luckily, there are some things that you can think about as you begin. Figure 5.1 breaks the process down into steps.

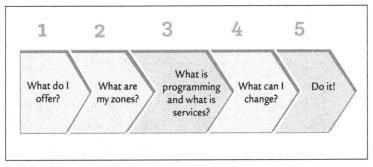

Figure 5.1. Where to begin making a difference.

What Do I Offer?

Ask, what does my library offer that will give students a better experience than the classroom? Libraries can offer students different opportunities to experience the content of the classroom. What is it that will make the biggest impact that can't or doesn't happen in classrooms in your school? Maybe what you can offer is a makerspace, an audio/video production studio, a quiet place to study, or even virtual reality experiences. Defining that differentiator is an important piece.

What Are My Zones?

Understand the different zones that are present in your library. In her ISTE book, *Reimagining Library Spaces: Transform Your Space on Any Budget* (2016), Diana Rendina discusses active learning theory and defines some of the spaces (or zones) that are often found in libraries. We like the active learning model because of the flexibility that it provides the librarian and the school community. Even if you use another model, understanding how your library is set up (or how you want it to be set up) can go a long way towards understanding how the space is used. We recommend actually drawing out a map of your space and defining each space and its usage.

ACTIVE LEARNING THEORY ZONES

* Large group
* Small group
* Quiet or study

* Community
* Technology-rich
* Creation and exploration

(Adapted from Redina, 2016)

Programming vs. Services

Identify the difference between the services and the programming you offer to your school community. We define programming as anything that is of a curricular focus and facilitates student learning. Services are those things that you offer to help others. It's a blurry line and sometimes, certain things may live in both services and programming, but identifying those tasks are important. See Table 5.1 for an example.

It's not that one of these is more important than the other, you just need to be clear about what the topic is.

Table 5.1 | Programming vs. Services.

PROGRAMMING	SERVICES
• Research	• Providing databases
• Media Literacy	• Supplying Breakout Boxes for teachers
• Breakout Box (if part of a lesson)	• Shelving books
• Material curation for teachers	• Student supervision
• Hour of Code	• Checking out books

What Can I Change?

Plan for change. Once you know your goals, zones, and the difference between your programming and your services, decide how to sequence the changes that you want to make. For this, we use a planning document (found at **tiny.cc/owls2y**) that helps to define our course of action to see what is feasible based on different time frames. For instance, what change could you make tomorrow that will have an impact on your space? What about your programming or your services? You can't do it all at once so planning and visioning becomes essential. In the planning document in Table 5.2 you probably won't fill all the boxes, but it does give you a sense of where you are now and where you want to end up.

Table 5.2 | Library Change Management Planning

TIME PERIOD	ZONE	SERVICE	PROGRAMMING
Example:	*Tomorrow I could declutter an area that will create a new zone for student collaboration.*	*Next week I could send out a flyer advertising our virtual spaces in terms of public library access, databases, and BYOD wifi connection.*	*Next semester I could reach out to a curriculum coordinator and inquire about the integration of technology in various units and share resources, tools, and experiences that offered through the library.*
Tomorrow:			
Next week:			
Next month:			
Next semester:			
Next year:			

Do It!

You have a plan, your ideas, and your direction. Now you have to make it happen.

Creating Impact

As you move on from this book, we want to leave you with one last thought: We are all educators because we want to have an impact on the students that we teach, and on society as a whole. We want to leave the world a better place through education, and we want to share our love for learning with our communities. As you go about your day-to-day work, analyze your decisions to insure you are leading in productive ways. You will always be busy. Someone—a student, teacher, administrator, or another member of the school community—will need or want something from you. How you respond to those moments defines leadership. If you say "yes" to everything, you will get bogged down in tasks and work that doesn't create impact. Be a leader and make decisions based on what you can influence and how you can best lead.

At this point, it seems prudent to point out that refocusing your priorities should be a gradual change in your approach. What we don't want is for you to immediately switch from being someone everyone can count on to someone everyone can count on to say "no." You will have to do some work up front to define and communicate your goals while, at the same time, making sure those goals support the overall direction of the organization and any initiatives currently being implemented or planned. It will require flexibility, patience, and strategy. If you are careful about the decisions you make, it can lead to great results for your school community.

Leading from the Library

Writing this book caused both of us to reflect on our practices, strategies, and partnerships that we rely on to keep our own programs moving forward. We have analyzed what it means to be a leader in the digital age, and we recognize that the changes happening in today's technological and educational landscapes can be both uncomfortable and unnerving. But we are more convinced than ever that your work is vital. Leadership is not a destination; you will never "arrive." Enjoy the journey, and be the force for change that is needed in our schools. Embrace that role as a leader from the library.

References

American Association of School Librarians. (n.d). *What is advocacy?* Retrieved from www.ala.org/aasl/advocacy/definitions

Alliance for Excellent Education. (n.d). *Future ready schools.* Retrieved from www.futureready.org

Follett Learning. (2015). Project Connect. Retrieved from www2.follettlearning.com/projectconnect

Kolb, L. (2017). *Learning first, technology second: The educator's guide to designing authenic lessons.* Eugene, OR: International Society for Technology in Education.

Lessig, L. (2008). *Remix: Making art and commerce thrive in the hybrid economy.* New York, N.Y.: Penguin Group.

Lindskog, K. (2018, March). *Analyze this, market that.* Paper presented at Missouri Association of School Librarians Spring Conference, Osage Beach, MO.

Perez, S. (2018). *Twitch now as 27K+ partners and 150K+ affiliates making money from their videos.* Retrieved from www.techcrunch.com/2018/02/06/twitch-now-has-27k-partners-and-150k-affiliates-making-money-from-their-videos/

Redina, D. (2017). *Reimagining Library Spaces: Transform Your Space on Any Budget.* International Society for Technology in Education: Eugene, OR.

Sheninger, E., & Murray, T. (2017). *Learning transformed: Eight keys to designing tomorrow's schools, today.* Alexandria, VA: ASCD.

TEDx. (2016, June 7). *Changing the conversation about librarians* [Video file]. Retrieved from www.youtube.com/watch?v=IniFUB7worY

U.S. Department of Education. (2017). *Reimagining the role of technology in education: 2017 national educational technology plan update.* Washington, D.C.: Office of Educational Technology.

Zmuda, A., & Harada, V. (2008). *Librarians as learning specialists: Meeting the learning imperative for the 21st century.* Westport, CT: Libraries Unlimited.

Resources

American Association of School Librarians 2017 Standards (standards.aasl.org)

Future Ready Librarian Framework (futureready.org/program-overview/librarians)

Project Connect (www2.follettlearning.com/projectconnect)

National Council of Teachers of English Definition of 21st Century Literacies (ncte.org/statement/21stcentdefinition)

National Council of Teachers of English Framework for 21st Century Curriculum and Assessment (ncte.org/governance/21stcenturyframework)

APPENDIX A

ISTE Standards

ISTE Standards for Educators

The ISTE Standards for Educators are your road map to helping students become empowered learners. These standards will deepen your practice, promote collaboration with peers, challenge you to rethink traditional approaches and prepare students to drive their own learning.

Empowered Professional

1. Learner

Educators continually improve their practice by learning from and with others and exploring proven and promising practices that leverage technology to improve student learning. Educators:

    a. Set professional learning goals to explore and apply pedagogical approaches made possible by technology and reflect on their effectiveness.

    b. Pursue professional interests by creating and actively participating in local and global learning networks.

    c. Stay current with research that supports improved student learning outcomes, including findings from the learning sciences.

2. Leader

Educators seek out opportunities for leadership to support student empowerment and success and to improve teaching and learning. Educators:

a. Shape, advance and accelerate a shared vision for empowered learning with technology by engaging with education stakeholders.

b. Advocate for equitable access to educational technology, digital content and learning opportunities to meet the diverse needs of all students.

c. Model for colleagues the identification, exploration, evaluation, curation and adoption of new digital resources and tools for learning.

3. Citizen

Educators inspire students to positively contribute to and responsibly participate in the digital world. Educators:

a. Create experiences for learners to make positive, socially responsible contributions and exhibit empathetic behavior online that build relationships and community.

b. Establish a learning culture that promotes curiosity and critical examination of online resources and fosters digital literacy and media fluency.

c. Mentor students in safe, legal and ethical practices with digital tools and the protection of intellectual rights and property.

d. Model and promote management of personal data and digital identity and protect student data privacy.

Learning Catalyst

4. Collaborator

Educators dedicate time to collaborate with both colleagues and students to improve practice, discover and share resources and ideas, and solve problems. Educators:

a. Dedicate planning time to collaborate with colleagues to create authentic learning experiences that leverage technology.

b. Collaborate and co-learn with students to discover and use new digital resources and diagnose and troubleshoot technology issues.

c. Use collaborative tools to expand students' authentic, real-world learning experiences by engaging virtually with experts, teams and students, locally and globally.

d. Demonstrate cultural competency when communicating with students, parents and colleagues and interact with them as co-collaborators in student learning.

5. Designer

Educators design authentic, learner-driven activities and environments that recognize and accommodate learner variability. Educators:

a. Use technology to create, adapt and personalize learning experiences that foster independent learning and accommodate learner differences and needs.

b. Design authentic learning activities that align with content area standards and use digital tools and resources to maximize active, deep learning.

c. Explore and apply instructional design principles to create innovative digital learning environments that engage and support learning.

6. Facilitator

Educators facilitate learning with technology to support student achievement of the 2016 ISTE Standards for Students. Educators:

a. Foster a culture where students take ownership of their learning goals and outcomes in both independent and group settings.

b. Manage the use of technology and student learning strategies in digital platforms, virtual environments, hands-on makerspaces or in the field.

c. Create learning opportunities that challenge students to use a design process and computational thinking to innovate and solve problems.

d. Model and nurture creativity and creative expression to communicate ideas, knowledge or connections.

7. Analyst

Educators understand and use data to drive their instruction and support students in achieving their learning goals. Educators:

a. Provide alternative ways for students to demonstrate competency and reflect on their learning using technology.

b. Use technology to design and implement a variety of formative and summative assessments that accommodate learner needs, provide timely feedback to students and inform instruction.

c. Use assessment data to guide progress and communicate with students, parents and education stakeholders to build student self-direction.

ISTE Standards for Education Leaders

The ISTE Standards for Education Leaders guide administrators in supporting digital age learning, creating technology-rich learning environments and leading the transformation of the educational landscape.

1. Equity and Citizenship Advocate

Leaders use technology to increase equity, inclusion, and digital citizenship practices. Education leaders:

a. Ensure all students have skilled teachers who actively use technology to meet student learning needs.

b. Ensure all students have access to the technology and connectivity necessary to participate in authentic and engaging learning opportunities.

c. Model digital citizenship by critically evaluating online resources, engaging in civil discourse online and using digital tools to contribute to positive social change.

d. Cultivate responsible online behavior, including the safe, ethical and legal use of technology.

2. Visionary Planner

Leaders engage others in establishing a vision, strategic plan and ongoing evaluation cycle for transforming learning with technology. Education leaders:

a. Engage education stakeholders in developing and adopting a shared vision for using technology to improve student success, informed by the learning sciences.

b. Build on the shared vision by collaboratively creating a strategic plan that articulates how technology will be used to enhance learning.

    c. Evaluate progress on the strategic plan, make course corrections, measure impact and scale effective approaches for using technology to transform learning.

    d. Communicate effectively with stakeholders to gather input on the plan, celebrate successes and engage in a continuous improvement cycle.

    e. Share lessons learned, best practices, challenges and the impact of learning with technology with other education leaders who want to learn from this work.

3. **Empowering Leader**

Leaders create a culture where teachers and learners are empowered to use technology in innovative ways to enrich teaching and learning. Education leaders:

    a. Empower educators to exercise professional agency, build teacher leadership skills and pursue personalized professional learning.

    b. Build the confidence and competency of educators to put the ISTE Standards for Students and Educators into practice.

    c. Inspire a culture of innovation and collaboration that allows the time and space to explore and experiment with digital tools.

    d. Support educators in using technology to advance learning that meets the diverse learning, cultural, and social-emotional needs of individual students.

    e. Develop learning assessments that provide a personalized, actionable view of student progress in real time.

4. Systems Designer

Leaders build teams and systems to implement, sustain and continually improve the use of technology to support learning. Education leaders:

a. Lead teams to collaboratively establish robust infrastructure and systems needed to implement the strategic plan.

b. Ensure that resources for supporting the effective use of technology for learning are sufficient and scalable to meet future demand.

c. Protect privacy and security by ensuring that students and staff observe effective privacy and data management policies.

d. Establish partnerships that support the strategic vision, achieve learning priorities and improve operations.

5. Connected Learner

Leaders model and promote continuous professional learning for themselves and others. Education leaders:

a. Set goals to remain current on emerging technologies for learning, innovations in pedagogy and advancements in the learning sciences.

b. Participate regularly in online professional learning networks to collaboratively learn with and mentor other professionals.

c. Use technology to regularly engage in reflective practices that support personal and professional growth.

d. Develop the skills needed to lead and navigate change, advance systems and promote a mindset of continuous improvement for how technology can improve learning.

ISTE Standards for Education Leaders, ©2018, ISTE® (International Society for Technology in Education), iste.org. All rights reserved.

Index

Page numbers followed by "t" and "f" indicate tables and figures.

Like What You Read?
We'd Love to Hear from You!

If you enjoyed this ISTE book, please consider leaving a review on Amazon or Barnes & Noble.

Want to connect?
Mention this book on social media and follow ISTE on Twitter @iste, Facebook @ISTEconnects, or Instagram @isteconnects.

Have a burning question or suggestion for us?
Email us at books@iste.org.

Your feedback helps ISTE continue to bring you the best possible resources for teaching and learning in the digital age. Thank you!

CPSIA information can be obtained
at www.ICGtesting.com
Printed in the USA
JSHW051918080721
16692JS00003B/187